MANAGING ATTENTION AND LEARNING DISORDERS

Managing
Attention
&Learning
Disorders

Super Survival Strategies

Elaine McEwan

Harold Shaw Publishers
Wheaton, Illinois

Acknowlegement is made to the following for permission to use copyrighted material:

Unless otherwise indicated, all Bible quotations are taken from the *Holy Bible, King James Version.*

Scripture quotations marked NLT are taken from the *Holy Bible,* New Living Translation, copyright ©1996. Used by permission of Tyndale House Publishers, Inc., Wheaton, Illinois 60189. All rights reserved.

The quote from Eileen Simpson in chapter 1 is taken from *Reversals: A Personal Account of Victory Over Dyslexia.* Boston: Houghton Mifflin Company, 1979. Used by permission of the author.

The Twelve Steps of Alcoholics Anonymous are reprinted in chapter 2 with permission of Alcoholics Anonymous World Services, Inc. (See also footnote.)

The material by Melinda White in chapter 3 is taken from "What Adults with ADD Would Like Their Friends, Relatives, and Significant Others to Know," *Challenge* July/Aug. 1994. Used by permission of the author.

The poem in chapter 7 is taken from Carol Deitering, *I Am a Pilgrim Child.* Used by permission of the author. Copies of the book are also available from the author at 1721 W. Klamath Dr., Tuscon, AZ 85704.

ISBN 0-87788-181-2

Edited by Miriam Mindeman and Joan Guest

Cover design by David LaPlaca

Library of Congress Cataloging-in-Publication Data

McEwan, Elaine K., 1941-
    Managing attention and learning disorders : a guide for adults / Elaine K. McEwan.
      p. cm.
    Includes bibliographical references (p.).
    ISBN 0-87788-181-2
    1. Attention-deficit disordered adults—Life skills guides. 2. Learning disabled—
    Life skills guides. I. Title.
    RC394.A85M38 1997   97-2831
                                                                        CIP

03 02 01 00 99

10 9 8 7 6 5 4 3 2

Contents

Introduction

I Really Do Understand

I always knew I was hyperactive. My mother did not send me to Sunday school because she was too embarrassed by my "wild" behavior. Rumor had it that I was retarded and my parents were keeping me in hiding.

I talked and moved nonstop—often running wildly in circles pretending to be a horse, until the day I ran smack into a corner and collapsed on the floor, sobbing as blood gushed from my head. The scar on my forehead reminds me of my youthful exuberance.

My mother was always in tears over the things I ruined—her new refrigerator scarred by my ice skates, her glass hurricane lamps shattered by a falling table, my aunt's antique clock smashed to bits. I left a wake of havoc and ruin. The bows and waistlines on my dresses were always ripped out. I sliced my thumb on the day of the big piano recital. Clumsy did not begin to describe me. I tore moldings off the garage door as I learned to back out of the narrow opening. But somehow through all of this, my parents affirmed and encouraged me.

When I was six, I started working for my father in his grocery store. I stocked shelves, put potatoes in ten-pound bags, and swept the front porch. My parents kept me busy every waking hour. Later, when my father bought a department store, I began working there at the age of twelve—marking merchandise, straightening piles of blue jeans, and assisting customers. My confidence grew as I learned to sell overalls to farmers and fit babies for their first pair of shoes.

From the beginning I drove the teacher in my one-room schoolhouse to distraction with my constant interruptions and hyperactivity. But she always managed to couch her report-card comments positively: "Elaine needs a hobby to keep her occupied" or "Elaine's energy needs to be channeled into positive interests." She stopped short of asking me to quit bugging her.

I was always finished first, so she put me to work helping others, even if they were older. When I moved into the upper elementary grades, my energies were put to work in administrative tasks—answering the telephone, running the mimeograph machine, grading papers, and straightening out storage closets. These chores, while contributing little to my academic skills, were excellent preparation for my later administrative career.

I gradually learned to sit in the front of the classroom, keep my mouth shut, and keep my hands busy taking copious notes. Classmates knew that I wrote down everything the teacher said—even the jokes. I started studying and organizing for exams weeks in advance. I knew my weaknesses well and learned to compensate for them.

Fortunately, I had a lot of love and reinforcement along the way. I believed that I could do or be anything I wanted to be. My home was organized and structured. Expectations were high, and nonsense was not tolerated. Today, I might be diagnosed as having ADHD. But in the late forties, I was simply a child with a lot of energy that needed to be channeled. I learned from personal experience what children with ADHD need.

Then, as a fifth-grade teacher in the sixties, I provided structure, organization, expectations, good home-school communication, hands-on learning, and a fast-paced and adventuresome day for all of my students, many of them with attention and learning disorders. When one approach failed to work, I tried another. There was no child who could not learn and thrive in my classroom. As an elementary school principal in the eighties, I continued to believe that all children could succeed in school. I had a special empathy for those children who were diagnosed with attention and learning disorders.

Because of my own success in school, I had always automatically rejected the idea that I might have ADHD; I was just a high-energy person. Nevertheless, as I began to read case studies, interview subjects, and reflect on my own life (I am now in my fifties), a startling pattern began to emerge—not only was I hyperactive, but I was also quite clearly impulsive and distractible.

I have spent a lifetime developing strategies and learning to manage ADHD (quite successfully as I have mellowed into middle age). For most of that time I was blissfully unaware that my idosyncrasies, as painfully detailed by those who know me well, were actually part of a cluster of symptoms of ADHD. The list of arguments my dear departed first husband and I continued to have over the twenty-six years of our marriage always centered on a number of key areas. And each time we faced one of these areas again, the plaintive cry that inevitably made its way into our discussion was "How can a woman who is so obviously intelligent be so lacking in common sense?" I never had an answer.

◆ I could never remember to turn the flame down after I had started something cooking on the stove. Result: many boiled-over pots, scorched frying pans, and ruined dinners. Fortunately, I never burned the house down.

◆ I was never able to gracefully leave a party. Even when we had decided ahead of time on our departure target, I was always talking to just one more person and saying thank you to the hostess one more time.

◆ I always seemed to have fifteen projects going at the same time. Even though I may have mentally scheduled dinner for six o'clock in the evening, I usually would forget to get something out of the freezer in time; we would end up going out.

◆ I never wanted to read the directions or take time to plan a project. I wanted it done immediately and the faster the better. Consequently, I often launched into something on my own, wreaking havoc wherever I laid my brush or applied my hammer. Even as my mind was saying no, my busy hands were putting together the crib or washing the second-story windows on my own.

◆ My husband and I constantly missed each other when I was supposed to meet him at the commuter railroad. I would be in the wrong place at the wrong time and totally confused as to how it had happened. Even when I wrote our plans down, I sometimes felt as though he were deliberately changing the arrival times to confuse me.

◆ I always ran at least ten paces in front of him until he reminded me that we were together. A romantic stroll was out of the question. I did not know how to stroll.

◆ When I started a project (homework for one of the courses I was inevitably enrolled in or a sewing venture), I could not bring myself to stop. I worked at a frenzied pace until I dropped the task, exhausted and frustrated that I had been unable to finish, but still incapable of sleeping for hours.

◆ I often impulsively agreed with others to do things without first discussing plans with my husband as I'd promised to do at least a hundred times.

◆ I recklessly disregarded the rules of safety by standing on chairs, climbing to the top rung of the ladder, sticking my hand in the chute of a running lawn mower, and other fooolish actions. Afterwards I always felt more distressed by my stupidity than by the abrasions on my back, my twisted ankle, or the bruises on my fingers.

For too many years, I believed that I was always right. I found my husband obsessed with safety, too deliberate in his decisions regarding purchases, and hypercritical beyond belief. I was defensive; I was angry; I argued. But we hung together, even though it was rocky at times, and I slowly began to see the wisdom of his ways.

I developed strategies for remembering and worked to curb my impulsivity and impatience. I recognized that if I was going to succeed in management and administration, I needed the ability to listen and admit my mistakes. My husband recognized my need for constant change and challenge, and he supported my return to school for a doctorate. Although life was stressful as we juggled multiple schedules and my periodic study binges, our children and our marriage survived and even thrived.

The amazing thing was that through it all I managed to keep my self-esteem intact. I realized that no one I knew was able to accomplish as much as I could in as short a time. I continue to have energy to burn and enthusiasm galore. In my professional life as an educational administrator, I have been able to motivate students and teachers to do things they never believed possible. I always have at least a dozen exciting projects on my to-do list, and I am having a great time doing it all. I realized as I began writing this book that not nearly enough has been written about the benefits of ADHD, of which I believe there are many.

Over the years I have developed countless strategies for succeeding in a world that functions best with schedules, organization, and structure. I have become an organized and effective administrator, giving advice on time management and writing books on instructional leadership and decision making. Most importantly, however, I have come through all this liking myself. I have learned how to relax and have fun, how to express my needs to those with whom I live, and how to prioritize and pay attention to the important things in life. My faith is strong, my mind is expanding, and I am learning and growing every day. I feel the best is still ahead.

This book contains the best of what I, and others with attention and learning disorders, have learned about how to cope with and even surmount our impulsivity, hyperactivity, distractibility, memory and study problems, and reading difficulties. There are many published volumes that contain detailed technical information about symptoms, diagnosis, and medication, but I have written this book to provide you with practical and workable strategies to help you deal more productively with your personal, family, work, or school life.

Because no two of us are exactly alike, you will have to experiment to find the strategies that work for you. I have found the resources of my faith particularly helpful in dealing with the challenges of ADHD, and I plan to share these ideas as appropriate throughout the book. Adapt these suggestions as they meet your personal needs.

Each chapter is arranged in ABC order, with an entry for each letter of the alphabet. You can read from *A* to *Z* or just browse at random. This book was written with you in mind—it doesn't beg to be read from front to back or even top to bottom.

Chapter 1 gives you the basic information regarding attention and learning disorders, with the scientific jargon kept to a minimum. If you are already well versed in these areas, fast-forward to chapter 2. It contains strategies for coping with the emotional and psychological fallout of feeling "lazy, crazy, and stupid." Chapter 3 aims to help you get along better with those you love by providing communication and listening skills, plus ways to more effectively discipline and at the same time live happily with your children.

Chapter 4 contains dozens of organizational and time-management skills to help you keep your life on track. Chapter 5 offers suggestions to help you survive the world of work, and chapter 6 helps you discover your personal learning style and fine-tune your reading and study skills. Finally, chapter 7 explores the important role the spiritual side of your life can play in healing the pain and disappointment that often accompany attention and learning disorders. Through my faith I have found strength to cope, resources to draw upon, and encouragement to guide me. I am honored to share my recommendations and experiences with you.

1

The ABCs of Understanding

Do You Have ADHD or LD?

Libraries and bookstores are full of books containing detailed and scholarly information about the symptoms, diagnosis, and treatment of attention and learning disorders (several dozen are listed in the bibliography). While that information is important and necessary, it does not always make for easy bedtime reading. So, I have organized this chapter in short, practical, and easy-to-read chunks of material that you can easily scan. If you have a yen to dig deeper, look at the bibliography to find what are, in my opinion, the best in-depth resources.

A DHD in Adults

Edward Hallowell writes in *Driven to Distraction:*

> I felt as if a boulder had been lifted from my back. I wasn't all the names I'd been called in grade school—a daydreamer, lazy, an underachiever, a spaceshot—and I didn't have some repressed unconscious conflict that made me impatient and action-oriented.[1]

ADHD is a neurochemical disorder that is genetically transmitted. It is biologically based and is not the result of poor parenting, lack of motivation, character weakness, stupidity, or psychological problems. ADHD generally affects three areas of people's behavior: attention, impulsivity, and hyperactivity. You do not develop ADHD as an adult; you either had it as a child or your symptoms are the result of some other problem. Between 30 and 70 percent of the children diagnosed with ADHD continue to have symptoms as adults.[2] Further, many individuals are not diagnosed with ADHD until well into adult life. They often stumble on the diagnosis when their child is referred because of behavior or school difficulties. In order for symptoms to warrant a definitive adult diagnosis of ADHD by a mental-health professional, the problems must be chronic (present since before the age of seven) or severe (affecting life in serious ways).[3]

Broken—If It's Not, Don't Fix It

If your life is okay, and you are coping with your attention and learning disorders well, you may not need a formal diagnosis—just a little fine-tuning here and there. But if you are experiencing anger, depression, addiction, chaos, disorganization, low self-esteem, anxiety, sexual dysfunction, reading and study difficulties, or job stress, you probably need to be thoroughly evaluated by a health-care professional. Telling your story to a skilled diagnostician may provide insights and help you to gain control of your life.

Causes, ADHD (Attention Deficit Hyperactivity Disorder) and LD (Learning Disability)

The most current scientific consensus is that ADHD is primarily an inherited condition. Although brain injury can cause symptoms of inattention, hyperactivity, and impulsivity, fewer than 5 percent of children whose records have been examined give evidence of brain injury. While environmental influences such as poor parental practices or family stress may increase the severity of the disorder or interfere with a successful treament plan, they do not cause ADHD.

A study by Alan Zametkin and his colleagues at the National Institute of Health in 1990 used a scanning technique called positron emission tomography (PET scan), which allows study of the brain's use of glucose.[4] The researchers described a significant difference between glucose usage in individuals with a history of ADHD and in those without such a history. Adults with ADHD utilize glucose, the brain's main energy source, at a lesser rate than do adults without ADHD. This reduced brain metabolism rate was most evident in the portion of the brain that governs attention, handwriting, motor control, and inhibition of responses. This study, along with others, has convinced researchers that ADHD is a neurological disorder.

Learning disorders, according to the National Joint Committee on Learning Disabilities, "are intrinsic to the individual and presumed to be due to central nervous system dysfunctions" and "are not the direct result of any external conditions or influences." Learning disorders seem to result either from hereditary factors or from specific problems that occur before or during birth or in early childhood.

Diagnosis of ADHD (Attention Deficit Hyperactivity Disorder) and LD (Learning Disabled)

> People wonder what is wrong with them and ultimately attribute their failings to defects in character or inner psychic weakness. Their lives seem to revolve around crisis after crisis and seldom do they feel truly successful in their endeavors.[5]

ADHD

Although diagnosing your own ADHD is quite possible, to obtain a definitive diagnosis, you must consult a professional. Many adults self-diagnose after accompanying a child with ADHD to the doctor, and about 85 percent of the time those who think they have the disorder actually do.[6]

Some individuals have been through a variety of therapies and diagnostic procedures trying to figure out what is causing the myriad of problems that plague them. Pat Hedstrom, a fifty-five-year-old artist, was diagnosed three years ago with ADHD by a psychiatrist who specializes in the disorder. Before that time, she had endured a variety of diagnoses and treatments, including administration of a drug to uncover possible sexual abuse (unfounded), sexual therapy, and hospitalization and treatment for aggression and rage. Here is part of the story she told to her psychiatrist:

> I've had a variety of symptoms over the years—confusion when I'm in a large group; angry outbursts when I am overwhelmed and tired; difficulty starting and finishing projects; difficulty focusing in church and small groups; and occasional depression.
>
> From time to time I wondered about ADHD, but because as a child I read so early and easily, I dismissed the idea. Grades kindergarten through eight were pretty easy for me, but as I progressed school became more difficult. My main problem was the factual material and memory work. College was difficult, but I found ways to compensate such as studying in the same seat in the library every day. For my foreign language class I translated a whole book in the margin to get through.
>
> After reading several books on the subject, I concluded that my mother has an extreme case of ADHD. My parents had a very difficult marriage, and my mother was very hard on everyone. My two brothers may both have it, and my two sons both have it in differing degrees.
>
> I've done a variety of creative things in my work life, including interior decorating. Now I do portraits to order, but I have a difficult time getting things done on time. I've always wondered how people got some things done so quickly and easily, but that just made me think I could do it, too, if I tried harder. The presence of deadlines is painful but helpful.
>
> I'm a very futuristic, creative, and visually oriented person. I was the architect for our home and many of my ideas, although they seemed far-out at the time, have ended up being an accepted decorating style now.

My angry outbursts were very damaging to me because they put me in a vulnerable position with plenty of guilt. Some abusive treatment by my first partner and my inability to set boundaries contributed to a divorce. The same pattern started again in my second marriage but after those years of misdiagnosis we were helped by working with a psychiatrist who understood and helped diagnose my ADHD.

Pat's story illustrates a number of important principles regarding the diagnosis of ADHD:

◆ You do not outgrow ADHD.

◆ The symptoms of ADHD can frequently and easily be attributed to other problems.

◆ It is never too late to get help.

◆ It is important to find a therapist or physician who understands ADHD.

◆ It is wise to read and learn all you can about ADHD on your own.

◆ You need to work in partnership with your health-care professional.

◆ Learn to appreciate the positives of ADHD such as originality, freedom with ideas, creativity with no boundaries, and boundless energy.

Learning Disabilities

Eileen Simpson, author of *Reversals: A Personal Account of Victory over Dyslexia,* describes her childhood:

There was something wrong with my brain. What had previously been a shadowy suspicion that hovered on the edge of consciousness became certain knowledge the year I was nine and entered fourth grade. I seemed to be like other children, but I was not like them: I could not learn to read or spell. Had my present friends, acquaintances, colleagues, and I grown up together, there would have been an abyss between them and me. The books they were then reading, I did not read. Their compositions merited gold stars, won prizes; mine were unacceptable. They were at the top of their classes; I was at the bottom. Throughout my childhood and youth the nature of my disorder remained mysterious to me and those in my milieu. When I was twenty-two it was diagnosed— not by a psychologist but by a poet: I was dyslexic.[7]

Even the experts cannot agree on exactly the right way to define and diagnose a learning disability or the best way to educate people with learning disabilities. If you suspect that you have a learning disability (particularly after comparing your problems with the symptom checklist later on in the chapter), seek professional help. Learning disabilities are diagnosed far differently from ADHD. Whereas the ADHD diagnosis relies almost completely on the individual's life story and anecdotal record, learning disabilities are diagnosed on the basis of a complete battery of tests. Insurance companies will often pay for testing, medication, therapy, and treatment for ADHD because it is listed in the *Psychiatric Handbook,* whereas the term *learning disability* (disorder) is not. For this reason, sometimes doctors use the terms *ADD* or *ADHD* on the billing sheet to make it possible for patients to gain access to insurance payments for testing and treatment.

Experts Who Can Help

"My son was diagnosed with ADHD, and his doctor, who is also my doctor, suggested that I might have it as well."

—*Stan Rogers, 38, trial attorney, ADHD*

The list of professionals whom you might consult for the exploration of and treatment of attention and learning disorders is very long. They draw on a variety of academic disciplines and perspectives, each one with its own language and treatment methodologies. Some specialize in children. Some specialize in adults. Some treat both. Choosing the right person can become a full-time job. Get referrals. Interview prospective professionals to determine their background and credentials. Here is the list (in no special order) of specialists who might help you:

psychotherapists   psychologists
counselors   neuropsychologists
pediatricians   school social workers
educational diagnosticians   family practitioners
marriage and family   neurologists
  therapists   school psychologists
psychiatrists   and educational specialists

F amily

Being part of a healthy family system is like having a million bucks in the bank if you have an attention or learning disorder. You can use your energies to deal positively with your challenges, and you will not be worn to a frazzle dealing with a dysfunctional family in addition to your own problems. If you are not sure what a healthy family even looks like (they do seem to be an endangered species in some parts), check out these fifteen traits identified by author Dolores Curran.[8]

If your family has them all, you may be eligible for an appearance on the "Today Show" or the network news. But most families are far more "normal," or "abnormal" as the case may be. At any rate, the list provides some good bench marks for which to aim. For more information on how to cope with attention and learning disorders in the context of your family life, consult chapter 3.

■ Fifteen Traits of Healthy Families

The healthy family . . .
 1. communicates and listens.
 2. fosters table time and conversation.

3. affirms and supports one another.
4. teaches respect for others.
5. develops a sense of trust.
6. has a sense of play and humor.
7. has a balance of interaction among members.
8. shares leisure time.
9. exhibits a sense of shared responsibility.
10. teaches a sense of right and wrong.
11. has a strong sense of family in which rituals and traditions abound.
12. has a shared religious core.
13. respects the privacy of one another.
14. values service to others.
15. admits to and seeks help with problems.

Groups, Support

It can make a big difference just knowing that you are not alone out there, that others share your frustrations and challenges. You can form your own support group or join one that is part of a national network. The national group CH.A.D.D. (Children and Adults with Attention Deficit Disorders) has local chapters throughout the United States. Locations, contact names, and phone numbers are available through their national headquarters. You can call them at 954-587-3700. For more information on other support groups, including groups for various learning disabilities, see the appendix.

Health, Mental and Physical

Attention and learning disorders can take a terrible toll on both physical and mental health. Depression, anxiety, and addiction are all too common in the lives of those with ADHD and LD. For more information on the mental- and physical-health dynamics of ADHD and LD, and for help on how to cope, see chapter 2.

I mpact on Daily Life

> "In a society that encourages order, I sometimes feel as out of place as a snowstorm in summer."
> —*Kristina Howard, 42, housewife and mother, ADHD*

Here are some ways that attention and learning disorders can affect your daily life:

■ You may find yourself daydreaming a lot.

■ You will start more things than you finish. Your closet is probably filled with half-finished projects.

■ The few close friends you have are often annoyed with your inconsistency and lack of follow-through.

■ Authority figures such as teachers, principals, policemen, and bosses really bug you.

■ You hate jobs with paperwork.

■ You usually make decisions much too quickly and only consider the consequences later.

■ You won first place in the "Procrastinator of the Year" contest.

■ You could paper your walls with speeding and parking tickets.

■ Your checkbook is a disaster.

J obs and Careers

Finding just the right job can be a challenge for someone with ADHD and/or LD. If you have one you love at which you are successful, rejoice! But if you need help with job-hunting strategies or suggestions for being more effective on the job, read chapter 5.

K nowledge

Become as informed as you can about your disorder. Read books, join support groups, gain access to chat groups on the Internet, or consult with your health-care professional about new developments. With increased understanding of the symptoms, diagnostic procedures, treatment options, and rights you are afforded in areas of education and employment, you will be empowered to maximize your potential. Once you are informed, educate your partner, family members, friends, and coworkers. In almost all cases, when people understand more about attention and learning disorders and how they affect your life, they become more understanding and supportive.

> *The forces that affect our lives . . . are often like whispers in a distant room, teasingly indistinct, apprehended only with difficulty.*
>
> —Charles Dickens

L earning
Disabilities, Definition

When I began teaching school in 1963, the term *learning disability* was rarely, if ever, heard in educational circles. It was not even recognized as a field of study until the late 1960s, and schools were not required to give special help to students with disabilities until the early 1970s. In 1973, however, Federal Law 94-142 defined learning disabilities and mandated that every school system provide special education appropriate for children with these disabilities. "Learning disabled adults (and children) are unable to store, process or produce information in the same way that the rest of us do, although they appear to have no physical, mental, or environmental handicaps to prevent them from doing so."[9]

Individuals with learning disabilities do not fail because they lack intelligence. In fact, by definition, they have average or above-average abilities. They do not have a low IQ and are not mentally ill. They simply have a difficult time learning in the conventional ways (particularly the ways that most schools are structured). A widely accepted term used to describe reading disorders is *dyslexia*. To some, the term is less demeaning than *learning disabled*, since the public often associates the term *disability* with retardation. Dyslexia, however, is usually part of a more general learning disability; only rarely does someone have pure dyslexia with no other learning disorders.

Mood Disorders and Other Things That Get Confused with ADHD and LD

It is not always easy to diagnose attention and learning disorders. Numerous emotional and physiological conditions mimic ADHD and LD and serve to confuse even professionals. All judgments should be withheld until a comprehensive physical examination has been done by a physician and a psychological evaluation has been completed by a psychiatrist or psychologist. Here are some of the problems that may be confused with ADHD:

anxiety disorders	bipolar disorder
thought disorders	depression

Even narcolepsy and sleep apnea can produce symptoms of impaired attention, memory loss, and fluctuating levels of alertness.

Newsletters

For the most up-to-date information on attention and learning disorders, subscribe to a newsletter. One I particularly like is *The ADHD Challenge*, a bimonthly publication. Jean Conner Harrison, the founder and former publisher, has recently sold the newsletter to Ralph and Lynn Koplowitz in West Peabody, Massachusetts. For twenty-five dollars per year, you can read articles on a variety of topics. A recent issue contained a "Guide for Couples regarding ADHD Adult Relationship Issues." To subscribe, write *The ADHD Challenge,* P.O. Box 2277, West Peabody, MA 01960, or call them at 800-233-2322.

O rganizations to Help You

The appendix is *full* of organizations and publications, but here are a few to pique your interest.

Attention Deficit Disorder Association (ADDA)
P.O. Box 972
Mentor, OH 44061
800-487-2282

Learning Disabilities Association
4156 Library Road
Pittsburgh, PA 15234
412-341-1515

National Center for Learning Disabilities
99 Park Avenue
New York, NY 10016
212-545-7510

Orton Dyslexia Society (ODS)
8600 La Salle Road
Chester Building, Suite 382
Towson, MD 21204
800-222-3123
301-296-0232

P ositives

"I like to transfer a dull day into a spectacular one by leaving my dishes half done and playing follow the

leader with my seven-year-old and his friends."
—*Kristina Howard, 42, housewife and mother, ADHD*

I am hearing impaired and can identify a variety of advantages that accompany this disability (e.g., not being disturbed by crying babies and barking dogs when trying to sleep). Those of us with learning and attention disorders must try to find the advantages in our situations as well. We must focus on the positives, never lose sight of our accomplishments, and find creative ways to encourage ourselves.

Here are some of the ways we shine, according to the experts:

◆ We can think visually.

◆ We have extraordinarily high energy levels and when focused can accomplish incredible amounts of work.

◆ We are creative, often in the form of artistic, musical, or athletic talents.

◆ We take on tasks and assignments that daunt ordinary people.

◆ We are tenacious, resourceful, intuitive, and warm-hearted.

◆ We are trusting (to a fault sometimes).

◆ We are sensitive.

◆ We are willing to take risks (sometimes beyond the boundaries of common sense or wisdom).

◆ We are spontaneous and uninhibited.

◆ We are fiercely determined to succeed.

Questions to Ask Yourself or Other Family Members

Remembering is a very important part of helping your health professional to determine whether you actually have ADHD. Ask a parent or older sibling to help you reconstruct your infancy, childhood, and adolescence. Ask yourself the questions in this list.[10] Affirmative answers here may be suggestive of attention or learning disorders.

Infancy

◆ Were you overactive in the womb?

◆ Did you have any developmental delays in walking, talking, etc.?

◆ Did you have a hard time with sleeping, eating patterns?

Elementary School

◆ Were you accused of daydreaming a lot?

◆ Did teachers claim you were not living up to your potential?

◆ Were you often sent to the office for talking out of turn or creating a disturbance in class?

◆ Do you remember having trouble fitting in with your peers or making friends?

◆ Did you ever visit a physician or psychologist for an evaluation for learning or behavior problems?

Adolescent Years

◆ Were your grades inconsistent?

◆ Were you so disorganized that it interfered with your productivity at school or home?

◆ Did you often fail to complete homework?

◆ Were you suspended or expelled from school because of bad behavior, getting into fights, breaking rules, or inappropriate behavior?

◆ Did you have poor study habits?

◆ Were you ever retained in a grade or did you drop out of school?

◆ Were your friends generally a younger age than you?

◆ Were you involved in numerous accidents and/or traffic violations?

R esources to Consult

In addition to the excellent books mentioned in the bibliography, consult these:

⊃ *Attention Deficit Disorder in Adults* by Lynn Weiss. Dallas: Taylor Publishing Company, 1992.

⊃ *Out of the Fog: Treatment Options and Coping Strategies for Adult Attention Deficit Disorder* by Kevin Murphy and Suzanne LeVert. New York: Hyperion, 1995.

⊃ *Succeeding Against the Odds: Strategies and Insights from the Learning Disabled* by Sally Smith. Los Angeles: Jeremy P. Tarcher, 1991.

⊃ *You Mean I'm Not Lazy, Stupid or Crazy?!* by Kate Kelly and Peggy Ramundo. Cincinnati: Quality Books, 1994.

Symptoms of ADHD (Attention Deficit Hyperactivity Disorder) and LD (Learning Disabled)

The symptoms/problems associated with attention disorders are many. To further confuse and complicate the issue, many of the presenting symptoms can be observed on a daily basis in just about anyone you would meet on the street. So, keep in mind that the severity, quantity, and onset (before the age of seven) of the symptoms are the critical attributes that separate someone with ADHD from anyone else. The ADHD Checklist can help you identify the common symptoms of ADHD that you may or may not have.

Many of the symptoms and problems associated with learning disabilities are similar or even identical to those associated with attention disorders. Individuals can have either attention or learning disorders, or they can have both attention and learning disorders. The difference between the two is that learning disabilities are believed to be actual permanent impairments in specific processes whereas ADHD is a neurochemical disorder. Because of its chemical nature, ADHD can often be treated with medication. The medical and educational community generally has not accepted a medical treatment for learning disabilities, believing that such disabilities can only be accommodated and compensated for through learning.[11] The LD Checklist can help you identify some common presenting characteristics of learning disabilities.

As you consider these symptoms, consider also their severity. Attention and learning disorder symptoms exist on a continuum. They vary in intensity, severity, and quantity from one person to another. Making generalizations about what people with attention and learning disorders are like is difficult. You are a unique individual, and your combination of symptoms will be different than those of anyone else with attention or learning disorders. Some readers may recognize aspects of their personality or resonate with certain characteristics of attention and learning disorders and yet not have the intensity, severity, and quantity of symptoms to be diagnosed. There is no point on a continuum where one passes from "normal" to "abnormal," or from "without" to "with," hence the difficulty in obtaining an accurate diagnosis. Everyone's mind wanders and everyone's discipline flags. And almost everyone can benefit from the suggestions in this book. But . . . not everyone has an attention or learning disorder.

ADHD CHECKLIST

Addicted

__ Do you drink four or more colas or cups of coffee per day?
__ Do you abuse cigarettes or No-Doz?
__ Do you use alcohol excessively?
__ Do you use drugs recreationally?
__ Have you ever experimented with hard drugs?
__ Are you addicted to alcohol or drugs?

Angry

__ Did you fight frequently as a child?
__ If someone yells at you, will you yell back?
__ Do you have a short fuse?
__ Do you become angry if criticized?
__ Is it impossible for you to remain calm if someone is angry at you?

Argumentative

__ Were you a difficult child?
__ Do you argue a lot?
__ Would your family and friends call you stubborn?

Depressed

__ Do you worry about the future?
__ Are you afraid you will never put all the pieces of your life together?
__ Do you have trouble getting out of bed in the morning?
__ Do you frequently feel overwhelmed?

Disorganized

__ Do you tend to be messy?
__ Are you overwhelmed when you have too many choices?

___ Are you unable to prioritize?

___ Do you shift from task to task without a plan?

Distractible

___ Are you easily sidetracked by unrelated things?

___ Do you jump from topic to topic in conversation?

___ Do you forget and misplace things?

___ Are you easily intimidated at the thought of a big job?

___ Do you have a tendency not to read or finish books, preferring magazines or newspapers instead?

Emotional

___ Are you moody?

___ Do you cry more often than most people?

___ Are you thin-skinned?

___ Do you have intense premenstrual symptoms?

Flawed Family Tree

___ Do you have a family history of alcoholism, depression, hyperactivity, or learning disabilities?

___ Does one or more of your children have ADHD or LD?

Forgetful

___ Do you forget appointments?

___ Do you misplace your belongings?

___ Do you forget to do important things?

___ Do you lose your car keys?

Hot-Tempered

___ Do you fly off the handle?

___ Have you ever quit a job or been fired because of an argument or for losing your temper?

Hyperactive

___ Do you eat quickly?

___ Are you very talkative, restless, and fidgety?

___ Do you tap your fingers or feet constantly?

___ Do you move around constantly when you are watching TV?

Hyperfocused
__ Have you ever become so involved in a project that you lost track of time?

__ Do you completely ignore someone who is talking to you while you are involved in your work?

Impatient
__ Do you hate standing in lines and waiting for people?

__ Have you ever walked out of a doctor's or dentist's office because you could not wait any longer for the appointment?

__ Do people who do things slowly drive you crazy?

__ If you cannot figure out directions in the first thirty seconds, do you give up?

Impulsive
__ Do you frequently interrupt other people in conversation?

__ Do you make decisions quickly?

__ Do you just dive in and figure it out as you go?

__ Do you say the first thing that comes into your mind without thinking?

__ Do you do dangerous things impulsively?

__ Do you often do or say things you end up regretting?

__ Do you spend money on things you cannot afford?

__ Have you made frequent moves and job changes?

__ Do you blurt out answers before the question is finished?

Inattentive
__ Do you have difficulty concentrating for long periods of time?

__ Do you find your mind wandering while you are reading or listening?

__ Do people complain that you fail to pay attention when they are talking?

__ Do you have trouble paying attention to details?

__ Do you have difficulty sustaining attention to tasks?

__ Do you have trouble listening even when spoken to directly?

__ Do you have difficulty following through on instructions?

__ Do you dislike jobs that require your sustained attention?

Socially Inept

__ Were you teased a lot as a kid?

__ Did you have trouble getting along with others as you grew up?

__ Did you always feel different as a child?

__ Were you called bossy as a young person?

__ Are you too blunt and critical?

__ Are you called inconsiderate by others?

__ Do you lack insight into how others perceive you?

__ Do you sometimes miss the social nuances in conversation and behavior?

Stressed and Anxious

__ Do you have a low tolerance for stress?

__ Do you react with anger, anxiety, and panic to stressful situations?

Time-Challenged

__ Do you procrastinate?

__ Do you have trouble being on time?

__ Do you tend to make too many commitments?

__ Do you keep people waiting?

__ Do you take on too many projects and fail to finish most of them?

__ Do you have time-management problems?

Tired

__ Do you have irregular sleep patterns?

__ Do you often have trouble falling asleep?

__ Do you feel tired no matter how much sleep you have had the night before?

Underachieving

__ Was school boring and frustrating?

__ Were you labeled unmotivated?

__ Did your grades in junior high and high school go down compared to elementary school?

Undisciplined
__ Do you have a difficult time sticking to self-improvement projects?

__ Have you taken up and dropped many different interests?

__ Have you been called lazy by friends and family?

Unemployed or Underemployed
__ Do you have difficulty finding and keeping jobs?

__ Do you feel that you are presently in a job that is beneath your level of competence?

LD CHECKLIST

Attention Problems
__ Are you distractible?

__ Do you have a short attention span?

__ Are you easily distracted by background noise or visual stimulation?

Auditory-Perception Problems
__ Despite normal hearing, do you have difficulty distinguishing between similar sounds?

__ Are you frequently unable to accurately interpret information received through the ears?

__ Are you acutely sensitive to background noises and unable to screen out traffic, whispers, or other sounds?

Cognition Problems
__ Do you have problems identifying the main idea of a story or speech?

__ Do you have difficulty with reading comprehension?

Dyslexia
__ Do you see letters incorrectly or in reverse order?

__ Do you fail to perceive some letters, words, or even whole paragraphs?

__ Do you confuse similar letters such as *b* and *d* or *p* and *q,* or confuse the order of letters in words, reading *was* for *saw* or *teh* for *the?*

__ Do you misspell the same word several different ways in the same composition?

Language Problems

__ Do you have poor listening skills?

__ Do you frequently mishear what is said or have gaps in what is heard?

Left-Right Confusion

__ Do you reverse letters and numbers when you write them?

__ Do you have a hard time telling the difference between your right and left hand?

Memory Problems

__ Do you have difficulty following instructions?

__ Is it hard for you to remember abstract material?

Motor Problems

__ Are you clumsy, tending to bump into things?

__ Do you have difficulty with your handwriting (e.g., poorly formed letters, inconsistent slant, words spaced unevenly)?

__ Are you disorganized in space (e.g., getting lost in buildings and becoming disoriented when a familiar environment is rearranged)?

Organization Problems

__ Do you have a hard time organizing information coming in through your senses?

__ Do you have a hard time keeping track of your belongings?

__ Do you have a hard time sticking to a schedule?

Sequencing Problems

__ Do you have trouble understanding or following directions?

__ Are you easily overwhelmed by a sequence of directions given all at once?

__ Do you frequently need to have information repeated?

Social Behavior Problems
__ Do you become easily frustrated in social situations and make inappropriate responses?

Symbol-Learning Problems
__ Did you have a difficult time learning phonics?
__ Do you have problems with basic math operations?

Visual-Spatial Problems
__ Is it hard for you to perceive or remember the proper sequence of letters in a word or numbers in a telephone number or other series?

T reatment

The treatment for attention and learning disorders is multifaceted. You might take medication, engage a tutor or coach, see a psychotherapist or family counselor, join a support group, or simply do reading and research on your own. Because of the complexity of the disorders and the variety and intensity of symptoms, you will need to act as your own case manager, seeking out just the right combination of activities and therapies to meet your specific needs.

U nrealized Potential

Now is the time to make up your mind to tap your unrealized potential. Read the next six chapters and "be all that you can be."

V ictory

Whenever I am discouraged by my deficits, disorders, impairments, disabilities, and handicaps, I read stories by and about those who have overcome theirs. They inspire me and assure me that victory over disorder is possible. The attention and learning disorders' Hall of Fame (my own invention) is large and impressive, but there is always room for another name to be added to the list—yours. Here is a small sampling:

Sarah Bernhardt
Cher
Winston Churchill
Sir Arthur Conan Doyle
Thomas Alva Edison
Enrico Fermi
Arturo Toscanini

John F. Kennedy
Florence Nightingale
Greg Louganis
Friedrich Nietzsche
Will Rogers
Charles Schwab

ell-Grounded

I hope that you are feeling well-grounded as you complete chapter 1. Well-grounded means having a thorough, basic knowledge of the subject. For more detailed information on attention and learning disorders, see the bibliography.

X -emplary

The individuals with attention and learning disorders who contributed to the research for this book by completing questionnaires constitute their own special Hall of Fame. They were able to overcome procrastination, family emergencies, final exams, difficulties with written expression, and various other obstacles to get the job done. I have changed their names to protect their privacy, but each one of them has my sincere thanks.

Y et

This simple word implies a future—still, even now, in the time remaining. You may have attention and learning disorders, yet there is the possibility of overcoming them. Do not delay. Take advantage of that *yet*.

Z ing

Webster's defines *zing* as a "lively zestful quality; something with vigor, force, and vitality." Sounds like a description of someone with ADHD! I hope that is what you will find as you read on. Enjoy!

2

The ABCs of Liking Yourself

Dealing with Feeling Lazy, Stupid, or Crazy

Having an attention or learning disorder can take its toll on the self-esteem of even the heartiest ego. Whether you are living with difficulties in learning and remembering, dealing with the addiction or depression that is a part of your ADHD, or handling the pain of rejection and failed relationships that often accompany learning and attention disorders, there are a variety of coping strategies available to you. They can help you increase your sense of self-esteem; bring positive changes in your physical, spiritual, and emotional health; and restore balance and harmony to your life as you understand your past and learn to talk positively to and about yourself. The strategies that follow are arranged in alphabetical order. Of course, I will not presume to tell you what is most important or what area of your life needs attention. Just remember, you cannot do it all at once. Where appropriate, I have suggested resources you can consult for more in-depth information about the strategy.

ddiction

"I no longer drink alcohol. I don't have depression. I can read now."

—*Marlene Jensen, 52, housewife, LD*

If you are addicted to alcohol, hard drugs (e.g., cocaine or heroin), tranquilizers, or amphetamines, seek professional help immediately. You are probably using these substances to deaden the pain of a life that is out of control. In addition to substances, some individuals are addicted to other things that on the surface may seem less harmful but can be just as destructive when used to avoid facing critical issues in a person's life. Examples include work, shopping, sleeping, cleaning, volunteer work, computer games, sex, gambling, obsessive relationships, reading, television, and procrastination.

You may adapt the following Twelve Steps of Alcoholics Anonymous as you deal with any of the addictions that control your life. Search for a Twelve Step group in your area and begin attending now.

1. We admitted we were powerless over alcohol—that our lives had become unmanageable.

2. Came to believe that a Power greater than ourselves could restore us to sanity.

3. Made a decision to turn our will and our lives over to the care of God *as we understood Him.*

4. Made a searching and fearless moral inventory of ourselves.

5. Admitted to God, to ourselves and to another human being the exact nature of our wrongs.

6. Were entirely ready to have God remove all these defects of character.

7. Humbly asked Him to remove our shortcomings.

8. Made a list of all persons we had harmed, and became willing to make amends to them all.

9. Made direct amends to such people wherever possible, except when to do so would injure them or others.

10. Continued to take personal inventory and when we were wrong promptly admitted it.

11. Sought through prayer and meditation to improve our conscious contact with God, *as we understood Him,* praying only for knowledge of His will for us and the power to carry that out.

12. Having had a spiritual awakening as the result of these steps, we tried to carry this message to alcoholics, and to practice these principles in all our affairs.[1]

B umping into Things

Kermit the Frog laments that "it's not easy being green." For those of us with attention and learning disorders, "it's not easy being klutzy." We run into things, knock things over, and hurt ourselves in a variety of bizarre ways. It may help just knowing that this is normal for us. But here are a few simple precautions you can take to minimize this characteristic:

⊃ Think and be aware before you move—shift the plate before you drag your sleeve in spaghetti sauce.

⊃ Arrange the furniture to remove obstacles from the traffic pattern.

⊃ Look at your feet from time to time to see if there is something in the way.

⊃ Finally, move more slowly and deliberately to avoid knocking things over.

C oaches

"My seventh-grade teacher was the first person to recognize that I wasn't retarded, a label I'd carried to that point in my life because of my retarded mother and two siblings. This man believed in me and showed me how I could succeed. He absolutely turned my life around."

—*Teresa Lorenzen, 34, college student and mother, LD*

"Ruth is my learning specialist and friend. She taught me to be organized and to actually study for tests and do my homework. She also taught me that I was beautiful on the inside even though I was different. Ruth showed me who I was. I learned that I was smart and not dumb. Slowly, my grades came up, along with my self-esteem."

—*Jessica Beacon, 16, high school student, ADHD*

A *coach* here refers to any person who gives focused attention to help someone else. A coach may be a paid professional or a personal friend. A coach is any individual who meets with you several times a week to go over what is going on in your life. He or she may offer encouragement, prodding, or organizational assistance. Coaches may also function as tutors and mentors. Parents and spouses do not usually make very good coaches simply because of their emotional connection. Coaches enrich your life when they . . .

◆ recognize your true abilities, talents, and gifts.

◆ help you organize the "stuff" in your life.

◆ encourage and affirm you.

◆ help you prioritize.

◆ teach you how to do something you do not know how to do.

D epression

"I push myself so hard that I'm depressed, over-stressed, and I want to drop out. Then the cycle starts over."

—*Stan Rogers, 38, trial attorney, ADHD*

Depression is a frequent companion of those with attention and learning disorders. Symptoms include, but are not limited to

a low energy level
a feeling of sadness nearly every day
significant weight loss or gain
persistent insomnia or hypersomnia (sleeping too much)
no longer finding pleasure in favorite activities
crying jags

Depression is often associated with abnormalities in brain chemistry, including chemicals called norepinephrine, serotonin, and possibly dopamine. Here are some ways to handle depression:

➲ Seek professional help and determine if one of several types of psychotherapy may be effective for you.

➲ Consider using one of the medications (if prescribed) that affect these chemicals to assist you in "getting over the hump."

➲ Be prepared for the inevitable short-term depression that may occur when you have reached a major goal. Recognizing that this is part of your normal cycle of feelings will keep you from focusing on the negative. Take a few days to recharge (rest, exercise, eat nutritious food, and seek a change of scenery).

➲ Learn to say no. Depression is often the result of overwork and overload. Simplifying your life and removing unnecessary pressure can lift your spirits dramatically.

➲ Draw on the resources of your own faith using some of these suggestions:

1. Spend time reading the Bible or other inspirational readings and meditate on passages that will give you strength;

2. Express your problems to God through spoken prayer or prayers written in your journal; and

3. Draw on the supernatural power of your relationship to God.

Taken from *100 Ways to Overcome Depression* by Frank Minirth, States Skipper, and Paul Meier. Grand Rapids, MI: Baker Books, 1979.

Exercise

Exercise is powerful therapy for the symptoms of attention and learning disorders. I walk three miles every day and do weight training every other day. In addition to the physical benefits (reducing the incidence of heart disease, stroke, osteoporosis, cancer, and high blood pressure), regular exercise will give you a renewed sense of mental and emotional well-being and enable you to sleep more soundly. Frequently it also alleviates some of the symptoms of ADHD, such as anxiety and depression. Some researchers have hypothesized that endorphins (brain chemicals released during exercise) seem to help improve focus and concentration, but more recent research seems to indicate that the positive results of exercise are due to changes in the production of dopamine, norepinephrine, and serotonin.

Here are some suggestions to consider in your exercise plans:

◆ Choose the form of exercise that is most enjoyable to you (walking, running, racquetball, aerobics, biking).

◆ Try participating in martial arts—an excellent way to work out along with training for self-control and concentration.

◆ Vary your routine to keep from becoming bored.

◆ Schedule exercise at a time that fits in with your personal and work life.

◆ Exercise with a friend or your spouse to help you maintain a regular schedule.

◆ Avoid exercise that causes pain. This sounds so obvious, but many people believe that without pain there is no gain.

◆ Chart your progress. Give yourself a reward when you reach goals.

◆ Exercise in moderation. If you are impulsive about exercise, you will end up with injuries.

 ood

Preparing food has always been one of the most challenging aspects of my life with ADHD because it requires advance planning. When I lived alone I coped by always eating the same meals—toast for breakfast, McDonald's hamburger and fries for lunch, and cereal for supper. It was not the most well rounded diet, but it required almost no planning ahead. When I was cooking for a family of four, things were far more complicated. I had to shop, take things out of the freezer, and stop what I was doing to start dinner. I had a difficult time getting motivated for cooking. Consequently, we ate a lot of carryout (not necessarily fast-food) meals. These were healthy, relatively inexpensive, and fast. As I have gotten older and wiser I have changed some of my eating habits. Now I am down to my "fighting weight," my recent physical was perfect, and I feel good. Here are some of the hard and fast rules I follow:

■ Stay away from greasy, fast foods.

■ Enjoy the food you eat rather than wolfing it down while you are reading, working, or watching TV.

■ If you are tempted to snack on unhealthy foods, think of something else to do at that moment that will be healthier and more satisfying.

■ Find a menu plan and stick to it (the simpler the better).

- Read the nutrition labels that appear on nearly every packaged food. When I actually see how many calories and how much fat I will ingest from something that I do not even like that much, I find the power to say no.

- Plan and cook ahead.

- Eat at regular times.

- Eat several smaller meals each day to avoid feeling groggy and uncomfortable.

Losing Weight Permanently: Secrets of the 2% Who Succeed by Gregory L. Jantz. Wheaton, IL: Harold Shaw Publishers, 1996.

G rief

Upon receiving a diagnosis of an attention or learning disorder, some individuals experience an intense sense of loss at their unrealized potential. You must move through the passages of grief over this loss much as you would after experiencing the death of a loved one. Perhaps you will find it helpful or even necessary to move through the five tasks of grief in this list adapted from Lewis Tagliaferre and Gary Harbaugh's book *Recovery from Loss.*[2]

1. Acknowledge that your past is gone. You cannot reclaim it or relive it.

2. Feel (or experience) all of the results of the loss of that past (fear, anger, guilt, panic, jealousy, and depression in addition to the actual physical symptoms) and then begin to let go of them.

3. Substitute healthy activities and behaviors to replace the functions and roles that your disorder fulfilled for you. Find a new identity based on knowing that you are not "crazy, stupid, or lazy."

4. Detach yourself from your old self and make a commitment to invest in new learnings, new behaviors, and new attachments.

5. Reconstruct an integrated life from the remaining parts of your old life that you want to maintain.

H yperactivity

> "I feel like I'm exploding, and I can't get my body together; it's a sense of coming undone."
> —*Maria Shaw, 31, conductor and performer, ADHD*

Hyperactivity got many of us in trouble when we were kids. We were whirling dervishes, literally bouncing off the walls. We drove our parents, teachers, and friends crazy with our incessant chatter and impulsive behavior. Now that we have grown up, our hyperactivity may be less troublesome. We may have channeled it in more productive ways. But some of us are still jiggling and jumping. If your hyperactivity is still an issue, try these techniques to keep you active while you are doing other things.

◆ Work at a stand-up desk.

◆ Use two or more work stations so you can move from place to place.

◆ Fit your stationary bike with a reading rack.

◆ Chew gum while you are working (if you will not disturb others).

◆ Read in a rocking chair or porch swing.

◆ Have hands-on activities available (perhaps a game or toy) for those moments when you need to be moving but can't.

◆ Schedule regular breaks in your work.

◆ Use relaxation techniques such as deep breathing to slow down your body.

◆ Use medication if recommended by your health professional.

◆ Get plenty of exercise every day.

▐ mpulsivity and Inattention

> "It's like I'm standing outside of my body watching myself, but I cannot stop myself. I'm out of control."
>
> —*Maria Shaw, 31, conductor and performer, ADHD*

We impulsively say things, do things, and buy things. We cannot take the time to get advice before implementing our wishes and desires. We want what we want when we want it. We charge off in a new direction, seldom realizing that there is no one following us (either physically or psychologically) in our glorious quest. We are unable or unwilling to delay our immediate gratification in order to realize long-term goals. We are easily frustrated by having to wait.

There are no easy ways to decrease our impulsivity and increase our patience and forbearance. Hard work, perseverance, coaching, maturity, and medication will all help, however. And here are some other strategies to keep in mind:

⊃ Get advice from people you trust so you avoid making major mistakes such as quitting one job before you have another.

⊃ Get into counseling.

⊃ Do not get married until you have dated someone for at least a year.

⊃ Never buy anything that you cannot return.

J umping In

Interrupting others during a conversation or while they are busy working has been a big problem for me in my life; it is part of the impulsivity of ADHD. I have found that these strategies work (most of the time):

◆ Sit on your hands.

◆ Bite your tongue.

◆ Think before you speak.

◆ Count to ten.

◆ Ask the person who is speaking if he or she is finished.

◆ Temporarily disengage yourself from the conversation, particularly if you sense yourself becoming angry or frustrated by what is being said.

K nuckling Down

My Good Intentions

I meant to do it.
But I forgot.

Sorry I'm late.
Too much on my plate.

I have an idea.
But it's not quite there.

I'm almost done.
Does "almost" count?
—*Elaine K. McEwan, author, ADHD*

"Sorry this is so late. Had it [a questionnaire on ADHD] nearly completed, then had to set it aside. Forgot about it then."

—*John Griswold, 50, self-employed package designer, ADHD*

Knuckling down means getting busy, getting started, rolling up your sleeves, putting your hand to the plow and your shoulder to the wheel. But those of us with attention and learning disorders procrastinate. Our teachers, spouses, and friends (or we ourselves) have called it laziness, indifference, forgetfulness, work overload, or lack of motivation. Whatever name we give it, failing to get the job done is one of our major problems.

Psychologists suggest that one of the underlying sources of procrastination is fear—fear of embarrassment, rejection, or failure. But for many of us with attention and learning disorders, a greater source is the confusion we feel facing the sheer magnitude of even the smallest task. Achieving one small success can often be the breakthrough we need to throw off the shackles of procrastination. Choose a manageable goal, break down the task, and begin with step one today.

L istening

I personally have a hard time listening. My mind might be wandering elsewhere; I could be thinking of what I want to say in response; or I might be formulating the perfect solution to the problem. None of these approaches win friends or influence people. At best we are interfering; at worst we are uninterested. Here are some ways to be a better listener to your friend or partner:

⊃ Notice the attitudes and feelings as well as what the person is saying.

⊃ Be aware of body language and what it is communicating. Watch eyes, hands, and shoulders.

⊃ Try to understand the feeings expressed. Accept them as legitimate and neither deny nor minimize them.

➲ Listen between the lines for what is not being said but still being felt.

➲ Check out what you are hearing by restating it as accurately as you can, together with the attitudes and feelings you heard expressed. Try to use words that are different from the other person's without changing the meaning expressed.

➲ Do not respond with your own message by evaluating, sympathizing, giving your opinion, offering advice, analyzing, or questioning. Simply report back what you heard in the message, with the attitudes and feelings that were expressed.

M edication for ADHD

> "I use Ritalin when I need to work on one project for a long period of time. I do find, however, that when I am on the medication I go to another extreme. I not only dictate a letter, but I type it, address the envelope, make a copy, stamp it, and put it in the mailbox. On medication I am so focused that each project must be concluded."
>
> —*Stan Rogers, 38, trial attorney, ADHD*

Since ADHD is a disorder with a cluster of symptoms and not a disease, there is no specific cure. But medication can often produce dramatic improvements in concentration and attention as well as help in reducing impulsivity. There are two types of medications most commonly used for the treatment of ADHD in adults: antidepressants and psychostimulants. The goal of medication is to reestablish a proper balance of neurotransmitters in the brain. Consult one of many excellent volumes that discuss the pros and cons of medication in general, and the uses of specific drugs for various problems you may have in conjunction with your ADHD.

These principles should always guide your approach to the use of medication prescribed by your health professional:

◆ Beware of any health professional who will prescribe drugs for you based on your own diagnosis.

◆ Make sure that your medical exam eliminates other conditions that mimic ADHD.

◆ Keep a drug diary, noting daily symptoms and effects and when they occurred.

◆ Be patient and flexible as you and your doctor attempt to find the best drug and dosage for your needs.

◆ Communicate with your doctor often.

◆ Understand the limitations of medication. It will not improve your self-esteem or self-confidence, make you more organized, or solve any of your career, interpersonal, or emotional problems. You will have to handle all of those challenges the old-fashioned way—with hard work.

Driven to Distraction by Edward M. Hallowell and John J. Ratey. New York: Pantheon, 1994.

Medications for Attention Disorders: ADHD/ADD and Related Medical Problems by Edna D. Copeland. Atlanta: Resurgens Press, 1994.

N egative Self-Talk

Positive self-talk is important. Erase the negative talk that says, "I can't," and replace it with positive statements. Thomas Armstrong suggests substituting positive terms for the negative terms that may pervade your "inner vocabulary."[3] Although he is writing to parents of children with ADHD, the principle has application for adults as well. Consider the examples in this chart:

Instead of thinking of yourself as	*Think of yourself as*
hyperactive	energetic
impulsive	spontaneous

distractible	creative
a daydreamer	imaginative
inattentive	global thinker
unpredictable	flexible
argumentative	independent
stubborn	committed
irritable	sensitive
aggressive	assertive
attention or learning disordered	unique

O verfocusing

My most outrageous example of overfocusing, or *perseveration* as psychologists sometimes describe it, occurred one day during a sewing project. Rather than laying the project aside when fatigue set in, I worked late into the evening, eager to finally stitch the dress together. After midnight I achieved my goal, only to discover that the dress did not fit—it was so small I could not even get it over my head. The pattern was my size; I had carefully (I thought) followed every step; I was flabbergasted. Finally, my husband succeeded in dragging me to bed, assuring me that in the bright light of morning I would discover what had gone wrong and be able to fix it. I can still remember what a struggle it was for me to leave the project. I slept fitfully, still sewing in my dreams.

In the early light I jumped from bed and tore through the directions and bits of fabric. To my dismay I discovered my error—the dress design included a fitted bodice and waist formed of six different sections, and lost in the confusion of my sewing table were two of the six necessary fabric parts. When I added these to the dress, it fit perfectly, of course. I still perseverate from time to time, but maturity and discipline have given me a new perspective and a greater ability to stop, adjust, and move on when my approach to a task is not working.

P anic and Anxiety Attacks

Panic attacks create debilitating cycles in which the sympathetic nervous system aggravates the effects of stress a person is experiencing, leading to the emotional and physical symptoms of illness. Severe anxiety can cause prolonged bouts of sobbing, screaming, shouting, physical violence, self-mutilation, or even attempted suicide. During panic or anxiety attacks, hyperventilation can become extreme, triggering acute and crippling episodes that mimic the symptoms of a heart attack or stroke.

If you find yourself suffering panic or anxiety attacks, consult a professional. In addition, try to determine the source of your worry and take action accordingly:

⊃ If your worry is based on a decision you must make, first gather information, then develop a list of options, and finally make the decision.

⊃ If your worry is focused on the past, let it go. Realize that you cannot change what happened in the past, and refuse to wallow in regret.

⊃ If your worry is based on an unpleasant task or confrontation, take the action now. The longer you put it off, the stronger your worry will be. Just do it!

Anxiety, Phobias, and Panic by Reueau Z. Peurifoy. New York: Warner Books, 1995.

From Panic to Power: Proven Techniques to Calm Your Anxieties, Conquer Your Fears, and Put You In Control of Your Life by Lucinda Bassett. New York: HarperCollins, 1995.

Q uestioning Your Assumptions

Continually question assumptions about yourself that have been formed over time. Face yourself with this good news:

■ You are not unmotivated or lazy.

■ You are not deficient in some way.

■ You are not stupid.

■ You do listen.

■ You can change.

■ You can learn.

■ You can remember.

■ You will be organized.

■ You will not always have to feel about yourself the very same way that you do today.

Repeat a couple of these statements to yourself each day several times during the day.

R elaxation

Relaxation does not come easily to those of us with attention and learning disorders; we rush and hurry constantly. Nevertheless, it is an important skill to cultivate for health and happiness. Here are some suggestions that may help you:

◆ Intentionally build relaxation into your daily life. Take a break to read a magazine, walk around the block, or have a cup of tea.

◆ Create uncluttered space in which to relax. If your home or workplace is too distracting, relax somewhere else. I have found church chapels, small coffee houses, and public libraries to be wonderful places to relax.

◆ Do deep-breathing exercises.

◆ Play with your pets.

◆ Spend time in a secret retreat. When I was a child, the branches of an old willow tree were perfect. Now I retreat to my front porch to watch the sun set behind the mountains.

◆ Listen to music.

◆ Spend time with favorite friends.

◆ Watch clouds, birds, stars, or the sunset.

◆ Stop, sit down, and be aware of your own breathing. Do this any time during the day when you feel particularly harried.

◆ Take a nap.

The Relaxation Response and *Beyond the Relaxation Response* by Herbert Benson. New York: William Morrow and Company, 1975 and 1984, respectively.

S implicity

The whole concept of simplifying one's life flies in the face of the world view most of us have embraced—we are so easily convinced that more is better. Coping effectively with attention and learning disorders is easier, however, if you streamline your life. Cut down on the amount of stuff you buy and own. Reduce your activities and responsibilities. Remain focused on a few main goals in your work and personal life and regularly ask yourself if what you are doing at a given moment will contribute to reaching those goals. Try to do just one thing at a time. Stop reading while you eat and savor the flavor and texture of your food. Walk without talking and absorb the sights and sounds around you.

Simplify Your Life by Elaine St. James. New York: Hyperion, 1994.

> *Most men pursue pleasure with such breathless haste that they hurry past it.*
>
> —*Søren Kierkegaard*

Temper Tantrums

> "I struggled with outbursts over the years that were finally treated with Tegretol, and after several years of taking it, I was able to discontinue the medication. I don't seem to have trouble anymore."
>
> —*Pat Hedstrom, 51, artist, ADHD*

Managing anger is a major hurdle for individuals with attention and learning disorders. Here are some suggestions that can help you deal with the anger, aggression, and temper tantrums that well up inside you with frequency:

➲ Consult a knowledgeable health professional who may prescribe one of several medications used to control temper and aggression.

➲ Consult a therapist to assist with social-skills training or anger management.

➲ Learn to laugh more at yourself, others, and potentially frustrating situations.

➲ Use your energy to look toward the future. If you dwell on past hurts, failures, and missed opportunities, you will have no energy left to move forward.

➲ Get enough sleep. Lack of rest is a common cause of angry outbursts and verbal tantrums.

➲ If your anger is deep-seated and long-standing, face it openly and honestly. Talk about it with trusted friends or your counselor. Write about it in your journal.

> *Own less, do less, and say no.*
> —*Godfrey Goodbey*

➲ Beware of acting out any of your fantasies of revenge (harassing phone calls, anonymous letters, or hostile confrontations). This kind of behavior got you sent to the principal's office when you were in school, and it could have more serious repercussions now.

➲ Exercise to defuse angry energy.

➲ Try the popular time-out method used by mothers of out-of-control children. Send yourself to your room when you feel anger rising up inside you. Remove yourself from the scene until you have had time to count to ten or calm down.

➲ Pray this simple prayer as often as necessary: God, create in me a calm heart.

➲ As much as possible, eliminate frustrations, time wasters, and anger-producing irritants in your life.

➲ Identify and name the feelings that are behind your anger (e.g., grief, fear, helplessness, frustration, worry, rejection, fatigue).

➲ Identify what you need in your life (in work, at home, or from friends and family) to deal with your feelings more productively. Learn to communicate those needs in appropriate ways.

Underachievement

> "I was different. I always tripped and forgot things. I couldn't listen in class, so I'd talk to my neighbor. My homework was always a mess. I was lazy and naughty, but if I worked hard enough I'd be just as good as other kids. I knew this very well, because teachers had told me this all my life."
>
> —*Jill, 16, high school student, ADHD*

Perhaps you were described as an underachiever on one or more of your school report cards. The term generally suggests that someone has some ability but he or she is not using it—as if choice played a part in this achievement, as if working harder would make it happen. But working harder is not the answer. Understanding yourself and your disorder will be the key to unlocking your ability to achieve.

V isual Images

When I suggest using visual imagery, I mean picturing yourself in a certain way, for example, accomplishing something or behaving in certain ways. Athletes use it in this way, and it can be a powerful aid in helping people reach goals. Here is a personal example.

The four years in which I worked on my doctorate were an exercise in determination and grit. My twice-weekly evening commute of seventy-plus miles was often stressful. Tired after working a full day and fatigued by the demands of driving, I often fought the road every inch of the way. Then I discovered visualization. Each time I drove, I purposely imagined myself walking across the school stage and being "hooded" as I received my doctorate. I saw my husband and two children applauding me from the front row. I heard my friends and colleagues addressing me as Dr. McEwan. Through hundreds of miles of driving during fog, hail, thunderstorms, and blinding snow, I never lost sight of that vision.

W andering of the Mind

A sense of boredom and a constant shifting from one activity or thought to another are hallmarks of ADHD. Whether the distraction is internal (the thoughts that hopscotch across our mental landscapes and often take us to strange and unusual places) or external (the unusual hair color of the person sitting in front of us at church), we give every stimulus we receive an equal opportunity for our attention.

You can do some simple things to restrain your wandering thoughts. In addition to using medication, if prescribed, to help improve your concentration, you can make eye contact with and stay close to the person speaking. Some people also find that doing something with their hands—such as taking notes or making a braided bracelet—helps them to concentrate better on someone talking.

You can reduce external distractions during conversations by going to quiet restaurants. You can focus on family matters by turning off the TV during dinner.

Some people with ADHD find it easier to concentrate if there is something else going on in the same room (e.g., someone else studying quietly or music playing). One person likes going to a library to work and sitting where other people can see her. If she dawdles too much, she thinks that others will be watching her daydream, and that makes her concentrate better. Other people concentrate better in a room by themselves.

X-traordinary You

Author and theologian Martin Buber said in *The Way of Man:*

> Every person born into this world represents something new, something that never existed before, something original and unique. . . . Every man's foremost task is the actualization of his unique, unprecedented, and never-recurring possibilities and not the repetition of something that another, be it even the greatest, has already achieved.

Sit down with someone who knows and loves you and make a list of all of the things that make you unique and special as a human being. If you do not recognize your talents and strengths, you will fail to reach your potential. Discover what Rabbi Pesach Krauss calls "your own true song."[4] Find a way to tap into your unique gifts and talents.

Zigzagging

I do a lot of zigzagging in my life. I start out in one direction and then when distracted I abruptly change direction and dart off to do something else. Meanwhile, although I am accomplishing bits and pieces, my efficiency is grossly impaired. Discipline yourself to go in a straight line. An excellent example of straight-line functioning can be found in *Speed Cleaning,* a book by Jeff Campbell and The Clean Team.[5] Some of their recommendations for efficient cleaning have applications in many other areas of our lives:

■ Make every move count.

■ Use the right tools.

■ Work from top to bottom. Always. Period. Don't argue.

■ Pay attention.

■ Keep track of your time.

3

The ABCs of Coping at Home

Getting Along with Those You Love

"No one knows what goes on behind closed doors"—those lyrics from the country-and-western song by Kenny O'Dell[1] are a very apt description for what is happening in homes where attention and learning disorders reside. We adults can often compensate for and hide our attention and learning disorders from strangers and even friends or casual acquaintances. But, when we take off our public personas behind closed doors, there is no avoiding the problems that arise in our relationships with spouses and children. Among family we let our hair down and let it all hang out, and most of the time it is not a pretty picture.

When asked to describe their home lives, those who live daily with attention and learning disorders use terms like *chaotic, tense, irritable, energy-sapping, on edge, and all stirred up.* Multiply that by two when both spouses and one or more children have diagnosed difficulties. This is full employment for marriage and family counselors. That is, if anyone thinks to make an appointment, keep it, and then implement the suggestions made by the therapist. Your family will not turn into the Brady Bunch just by reading this chapter, but perhaps you will find one or two suggestions that might make life more manageable.

A ssistance

"I'll do it myself."
—*Elaine K. McEwan*

Only in middle age did I begin to understand the value of cooperation as opposed to independence and competition. I began to rely on others and ask for help (especially from family members). I learned to accept suggestions and constructive criticism along with the assistance that was offered. Of course you will need to learn, as I did, to set boundaries and reject what Sari Solden calls "toxic help," those negative messages that are sent by some people who are purporting to help you.[2] Gain the self-confidence you need to tell the difference between help offered by those who care for you and help offered by those who want to treat you like a child. If help makes you feel diminished, shameful, and incompetent, it is toxic. Walk away from it.

B irthdays, Anniversaries, and Special Events

Take time to celebrate the milestones of your life and those of your family and friends. In January I write down special dates in my calendar for the entire year. I make a note to send off a card one week before the event. On the day of the event, I place a telephone call. This behavior pattern is a relatively new one for me. For most of my life I made fun of people who remembered mundane things such as birthdays, mostly because I hardly remembered my own, much less birthdays of a flock of relatives. Oh, I would have good intentions, but somehow the big day would go flying by and then I would be too embarrassed to send a late greeting. I covered for my thoughtlessness by making sarcastic remarks about the phony greeting-card industry with its "trumped-up" holidays. Now, however, I have grown up a little, and I realize the importance of milestones.

C ommunication

Mary Ann Evans, whose pen name was George Eliot, wrote many years ago:

> Oh the comfort, the inexpressible comfort, of feeling safe with a person, having neither to weigh thoughts nor measure words, but to pour them all out, just as it is, chaff and grain together, knowing that a faithful friend will take and sift them, keeping what is worth keeping, and then, with the breath of kindness, blowing the rest away.

I wish I had practiced the following communication guidelines much earlier in my married life:

◆ Do not have major discussions when you are tired and/or hungry.

◆ Always take notes on important conversations (parent-teacher conferences, doctors' appointments, meetings with lawyers, budget meetings with your spouse).

◆ Keep a journal about issues in your life. Go back periodically and reflect on the things you promised to do or the ways in which you have grown and changed.

◆ When tempted to embellish, stretch, or downright rewrite the truth, be honest.

◆ Sit on your hands and do not interrupt.

◆ Try to stick to the topic. Conversational "birdwalks" (taking the conversation in a totally different direction) are permissible occasionally, but too many of them will annoy even the most patient friend or spouse.

◆ Use humor appropriately. Off-the-wall ideas and sarcastic remarks do little to help communication. Save them for a stand-up comedy routine.

◆ Learn to paraphrase what others have said to you.

◆ Make frequent eye contact.

◆ Focus on body language and vocal intonation to gain deeper understanding.

◆ Ask questions if you do not understand.

◆ Unclutter your mind before engaging in a meaningful discussion.

◆ Ask your spouse or significant other to gently remind you when you are speaking inappropriately (interrupting, birdwalking, blaming, being defensive, speaking sarcastically or critically, or monopolizing the conversation). Some couples use prearranged nonverbal signals to send such messages.

◆ Reduce distractions in conversations by shutting off the television, putting the children to bed, or hiring a baby sitter and going out for a quiet dinner.

◆ Try to keep from thinking too far ahead about what you want to say next. Focus instead on the speaker and his or her message.

◆ If you cannot accept constructive suggestions from your spouse (significant other) or if he or she refuses to give such suggestions to you, get a coach who can give you honest feedback on how you come across to others in conversation.

D iscipline

Discipline is essential in your family. Ignoring problems never makes them go away; it only makes them worse. Here are my ten commandments of discipline to be followed without fail:[3]

1. Thou shalt have clearly defined lines of authority. Your child needs to know who is in charge, what the rules are, and what happens when the rules are broken.

2. Thou shalt not "go with the flow." Your family needs predictability and routine. A fluid lifestyle at home will make it almost impossible for you and your children to accomplish work and school assignments.

3. Thou shalt always think and plan ahead. Overplan and you cannot go wrong. Help family members get ready for upcoming changes in schedules or situations. Rehearse and role-play behavior if necessary.

4. Thou shalt communicate. Be direct and assertive with your children and do not feel guilty about it. Permissiveness is just as debilitating as a harsh and punitive approach. Assertive communication exhibits patience, self-control, firmness, and clarity.

5. Thou shalt not obfuscate (confuse or muddle). Give explicit and direct instructions whenever you communicate with your child.

6. Thy consequences shalt be constructive and logical. Consequences that require restitution or contribution always work best.

7. Thou shalt be consistent. Enough said on this topic.

8. Thou shalt continually provide supervision.

9. Thou shalt not become angry, vindictive, hostile, ar gumentative, or physically abusive.

10. Thou shalt affirm, support, redirect, and educate.

Everything You Need to Know about Me and More

Share the following explanations about your disorder and its accompanying behaviors with your spouse or significant other, family members, and friends. Formulated by Melinda White, licensed marriage, family, and child counselor, these explanations may help those close to you understand and accept you more completely.[4]

⊃ When I don't complete a task I've told you I'd do, it's not because I don't care about you and it's not that I'm intentionally avoiding it. I get distracted by stimuli in the environment and often just forget. I do this with things I want to accomplish for myself as well. Please don't take it personally.

⊃ I agree that I shouldn't use my ADD as an excuse for not completing things. I am trying to find the right strategies to help me become more productive. Please be patient with me and realize that I need to find the method that best suits me.

⊃ When I say I will do something, I need to be given the freedom to do it my own unique way. My way may not make sense to you, but I need you to respect my differences and accept them as part of me.

⊃ I may be easily overstimulated by noises, lights, or crowded places. Shopping trips, parties, and large social or business gatherings may overwhelm me, and I might need to retreat to regain my equilibrium.

⊃ A full day of work or school may leave me feeling spent. I often need some "downtime" alone to recharge my batteries. This doesn't mean I don't appreciate having you around. I am able to be more receptive to you once I've had some uninterrupted time doing whatever helps me unwind.

⊃ I sometimes say the first thing that pops into my mind without stopping to think how it may affect you. I don't mean to hurt your feelings. My filter for screening thoughts isn't as well developed as I'd like it to be. Please let me know in a kind way if I offend you. It isn't my intention to do so.

⊃ I have developed the habit of saying yes to requests without really thinking through whether I can or want to do them. I am learning to say no when that is the best answer, yet this is difficult for me. After years of being criticized by parents, teachers, and partners, I learned to say yes to get them off my back. This was easier than admitting that I had no idea if I could or would actually do what I'd said.

Family Meetings

Family meetings are a wonderful way to build a feeling of teamwork and cooperation in your family. You can use them for conflict resolution, group problem solving, planning family outings, and many other tasks. All the people living in the family, whether or not they are related, constitute the family council. The meetings are regularly scheduled—nothing interferes with a family-council meeting, and conversely, family council does not interfere with any other activity.

During the meeting, all family members get to express complaints, ideas, or opinions and must hear those of the others. Every family member gets a chance to speak and may continue for as long as he or she wants. Family members can speak without fear of consequences. No one is to be punished for something said during family council. Everyone must be treated equally, regardless of age, and when a decision is made it will only be binding if all the family members who are present agree to it.[5]

Guilt

> "Don't worry about next week, next month, or next year. It'll be overwhelming. God only gives you enough resources to deal with today."
> —*Parent of two children with attention and learning disorders*

When you feel guilty, angry, and defeated, it is easy to fall frequently into the bad habits of nagging, spoiling, pitying, and babying your children. These are behaviors that will debilitate and disenfranchise your child. Remember, you cannot control your child, only your reaction to your child.

Household Chores

Chores are a sometimes distasteful, but always necessary, part of living in a family group. No one should have to be responsible for doing it all (and that includes Mother). Call a family meeting and decide how your family will handle the assignment of chores. Then follow these guidelines:

- Each member of the family is competent to contribute a fair share (e.g., to the accomplishment of chores, to a discussion of rules).

- Each family member is responsible for completing the assignment he or she agrees to do.

- The family agrees to live with undone chores or apply peer pressure until the person that is responsible does his or her job.

- Family members agree not to rescue each other if the chore is not being done by the assigned person.

- Agree that what is important is not how the job gets done (style) but that the job gets done.

- Assign chores based on ability, time availability, degree of distaste for the chore, and equitable distribution.

- Hire out the chores that you can afford to pay for and hate to do.[6]

Intimacy and Sexuality

Intimacy will not just happen, particularly if one or more of the partners has an attention or learning disorder. Maybe these hints will help.

◆ Plan for intimacy and conserve your energy to avoid fatigue.

◆ Take minivacations away from the chaos of home and family life.

◆ Make time for each other. Make dates and spend time away from distractions of family.

◆ Consult a sex therapist if you need help, but be sure to inform him or her of your attention or learning disorders.

◆ Tell your spouse what you like and do not like. Do not expect him or her to be a mind reader.

There are many behaviors that set up roadblocks to intimacy in a relationship. Do all you can to detour around these common ones.

■ Taking conversational birdwalks rather than focusing on listening and responding.

■ Using humor and sarcasm at the wrong moment.

■ Misinterpreting the words and actions of your spouse.

■ Feeling misunderstood and unappreciated.

■ Losing your temper and getting angry.

■ Being unable to sit quietly and concentrate on a problem or issue.

■ Talking on the run.

■ Falling asleep at the wrong time.

■ Raising your voice and waving your hands.

■ Tuning out and being unable to answer the question as posed.

■ Thinking about grocery shopping or golf during sex.

■ Being unwilling to ask for what you need.

oy

David J. Pine says in *365 Good Health Habits:*[7]

> If you have children, play with them! Instead of just watching them play, join them while they're jumping rope, riding a bike, or climbing on a jungle gym.

Take time for some joy each day. Tell a joke. Laugh at yourself. Smile at a stranger. Give someone you love a compliment.

K ids

> I've got a wiggle in my brain
> And I think I'll go insane.
> Cause I just can't stop
> The wiggle in my brain,
> Or in my knees,
> Or in my feet,
> Or in my toe,
> Oh no!
> —*Daniel Burns, 6-year-old with ADHD*

Chances are if you have an attention or learning disorder, one or more of your children also have one. In fact, many people are led to their own diagnosis through that of their children. Learn and grow with your children. As you discover strategies that work in your own life, share them with your children. Talk with them. Empathize with them. Encourage them.

L egalities

If you have a difficult time holding anyone (including yourself) accountable for behavior at home, consider using a contract. Lawyers, business firms, and teachers all use them to spell out expectations, and you will find that contracts can work in your home as well.

A contract must be in writing, and it must specifically spell out who will do what and how often they will do it. A contract contains the signatures of the family members who are involved, demonstrating their promise to consistently fulfill all of the obligations.

The terms of the contract must be appropriate for the age and ability of the family member and must include a description of the reward or consequences that will follow

> *Loosen up. Relax. Except for rare life-and-death matters, nothing is as important as it first seems.*
>
> —H. Jackson Browne, Jr.

the completion or noncompletion of the terms. The best contracts are positive agreements that will benefit everyone in the family.

Money

Money and finance are troublesome areas for many families with attention and learning disorders. Among the biggest problems are these: losing track of money, checks, and bills; impulsively buying unneeded things; spending too little time planning and too much time spending; and failing to talk about financial goals. If you are in over your head, put yourself in the hands of a financial counselor. If you have the discipline on your own, take the following steps:

➲ Cut up your credit cards in little pieces and start paying them off systematically.

➲ Leave your credit cards and checkbook at home when you go shopping. When you find something you think you want, write the item down on a list and think about it for a week. If you still want to make the purchase (and the item is still in the store), go back and buy it.

⊃ Stop reading catalogues and advertisements. What you do not see will not tempt you to buy.

⊃ Use a checkbook with a carbon for each check.

⊃ Buy a computerized check-balancing and check-writing program.

⊃ Have your paycheck and other regular payments deposited directly to your account.

⊃ Sign up for automated bill paying with utility and service companies. This will insure that your services are never disconnected because of nonpayment of a bill.

Your Money or Your Life by Joe Dominguez and Vicki Robin. New York: Viking Penguin, 1992.

N ighttime

Family life will be enhanced if you have consistent rules for bedtime that are strictly enforced. Fatigue is often responsible for arguments, misbehavior, anger, frustration, temper tantrums, and depression on the part of both children and adults. Sometimes the reason we sleep poorly is that we are preoccupied with concerns and worries. Our minds will not shut down, and the anxiety we create worrying about how we will function with so little sleep causes us to become even more wakeful. Here are some ways to ease your transition from wakefulness into sleep:

◆ Go to bed at the same time every night, preferably before eleven o'clock.

◆ Avoid nicotine, caffeine, alcohol, and sleeping pills.

◆ If you are awake for more than thirty minutes, get up and do something else such as read, meditate, or pray until you get sleepy.

♦ Use relaxation techniques to induce sleep.

♦ Take a nap during the day. The optimum time is between noon and three o'clock in the afternoon. Rather than making it more difficult for you to fall asleep at night, a restful nap may well cause you to be more relaxed and ready for bedtime.

♦ Eat at regular times during the day.

♦ Exercise during the day.

♦ Do not worry about a sleepless night here and there. Use it as an opportunity to pray or meditate.

No More Sleepless Nights by Peter Hauri and Shirley Linde. New York: John Wiley & Sons, 1990.

O pposite Attraction

My favorite occupation when killing time in airports is to watch the various couples that hurry by on their way to departures or fall into each other's arms at the end of walkways. The combinations and permutations are fascinating, and I often want to tap these couples on the shoulders and say, "Why did you marry each other?" Even from my limited perspective, many of them seem oddly matched. Those of us with attention and learning disorders are involved in our share of mismatches, and some try multiple marriages before discovering the right combination. If you are trapped in a relationship like any of the following described by Ratey, Hallowell, and Solden, seek professional help:

> *There's a cover for every pot.*
>
> —*My mother*

■ The pesterer (spouse without ADHD) and the tuner-outer (spouse with ADHD).

■ The messer (spouse with ADHD) and the cleaner-upper (spouse without ADHD).

■ The victim (spouse with ADHD) and the victimizer (spouse without ADHD). Or, the victim can be the spouse without ADHD who walks around acting like a martyr because of what he or she has to endure.

■ The master (the spouse with ADHD) and the slave (the spouse without ADHD).[8]

■ The caretaker (spouse without ADHD) and the helpless dependent (spouse with ADHD).

■ The warden/controller (spouse without ADHD) and the prisoner/controlled (spouse with ADHD).[9]

Problem Solving and Conflict Resolution

Conflicts and problems will not just resolve themselves. Use a structured method for resolving conflict in your family. Here is a model that our family has used and that I have used in my elementary school to resolve arguments between students. (When I was a single parent, I sometimes took my two children out to a restaurant to engage in conflict resolution. They were on their best behavior in a neutral setting, and this often served to bring a measure of calm to a potentially explosive situation.)

⊃ Call a meeting of the concerned parties and explain the purpose of the meeting.

⊃ Explain the ground rules to everyone.

⊃ Write down each child's feelings and concerns. Read them aloud to both children to be sure you have understood them correctly.

⊃ Allow each child time for rebuttal.

⊃ Invite everyone to suggest as many solutions as possible.

⊃ Write down all ideas without evaluating. Never skip this part of the process. Seeing each person's ideas written down will help defuse angry feelings and also help children see the ideas more objectively.

⊃ Decide upon the solutions you can all live with.

Quiet Times for the Family

> "I often find that simply slowing down long enough to give my children some extra feedback goes a long way toward helping them want to cooperate with me."
>
> —*Joan Griswold, 45, editor, mother of an adolescent*
> *daughter with ADHD and married to a husband with ADHD*

Schedule one-on-one time with your spouse. Do the same for each individual child and for your family as a group. Quiet bedtime chats and companionable silences are restorative and healing.

Rules

Every family needs to develop its own set of rules and put them in writing. The more carefully you spell things out, the less chance of hurt feelings and missed communication. Some rules are set forth by parents, and some can be decided in a family meeting. Here is a list of areas to get you started in thinking about what might be included in your family's list of rules:

■ which areas of the house are designated quiet zones

■ which possessions are off-limits for borrowing by children as well as adults

■ what types of communication and language are not acceptable

- how the telephone is answered and messages are recorded (Some families use a pad of carbonless message forms so there is always another copy if the first one is lost.)

- when television viewing is permitted

- who does what chores

- manners at mealtimes

- what happens when two people disagree about something

- where in the house people are permitted to eat and drink

- who sits where in the car

- who takes care of the car, the dishwasher, the answering machine, the lawn, the garbage, etc.

- what happens when someone does not like what is cooked for dinner

S ibling Rivalry

The only families I know that never face sibling rivalry are those with one child. So, be prepared and take a proactive stance.

⊃ *Create a family team.* Encourage shared decision making and cooperative family activities. Help your kids take responsibility for their actions. Build both group and individual accountability. Facilitate open lines of communication between family members, and model conflict resolution on a daily basis.

⊃ *Study uniqueness.* Make each of your children feel special and unique. Spend time alone with each child, listening to his or her joys and frustrations.

⊃ *Take personal inventory.* If you want to change your kids' behavior, you often need to start with your own. Do you have only a limited repertoire of things to do when your kids start fighting? Do you feel like screaming (and frequently act on that feeling) when your kids draw the battle lines? Are you playing favorites, interfering too much, or approaching problems out of harmony with your spouse? Take an inventory and get help if you need it.

‍⊃ *Nurture family.* Permit your kids to express their feelings. Spend time helping your children become nurturing, supportive siblings.

‍⊃ *Consider special needs.* If you have special circumstances in your family that seem to work against positive sibling relationships (such as a child with an attention or learning disorder), join a support group or seek out books and articles on the topic.

"Mom, He Hit Me!" What to Do about Sibling Rivalry by Elaine K. McEwan. Wheaton, IL: Harold Shaw Publishers, 1996.

T eamwork

Teamwork is the current buzz word, and the concept is just as important in family life as it is in business or athletics. In a family team, all agree to work together for the accomplishment of mutual goals, to participate equally, to take their share of individual responsibility, and to recognize and appreciate the differences in style and approach that each member has. If you want your family to function as a team, you will need to do four things:

1. Develop your own family vision and mission statements. Together decide what you want your family to be and do. Write it down and then work towards it.

2. Appreciate and affirm the uniqueness of everyone in your family—children and parents. No put-downs. No sarcasm. No ridicule.

3. Have regular family meetings to talk about your problems and issues.

4. Regularly do things together as a family.

U nderstanding and Empathy

> How far you go in life
> Depends on your being
> Tender with the young,
> Compassionate with the aged,
> Sympathetic with the striving, and
> Tolerant of the weak and strong:
> Because someday in your life,
> You will have been all of these.
> —*George Washington Carver*

Empathy helps others know that we understand and care about them. It means that we can see the world through another's eyes and understand why he or she behaves in certain ways. The next time you are ready to lose your temper and get angry at a family member, try these steps:

◆ Suspend your judgment just long enough to see the world through your spouse's (or child's) eyes.

◆ Sense the timidity, suspicion, anger, feelings of unfairness, fear, or confusion as if they were your own.

◆ Appreciate that no matter how unreasonable, irrational, or off-the-wall your spouse's (or child's) behavior may appear to you, to them it is quite reasonable and rational.

◆ Think about how your spouse (or child) has responded in the past to things you have said or done.

◆ See if you can predict how your spouse (or child) might respond based upon what you plan to say or do.

◆ Choose to act in a manner that you think will evoke the most positive response from your spouse (or child). Change your behavior rather than expecting your spouse or children to change theirs.

ision and Mission Statements

Vision is the driving force in your family, reflecting your image of the future based on your values, beliefs, and experiences. Mission, on the other hand, is the direction that emerges from the vision. The mission guides the day-to-day behavior of your family. Here are some examples of statements that are included in our family's vision statement:

■ Our family affirms the uniqueness and individuality of each member.

■ Our family believes that our spiritual growth is important, so we attend church regularly and have a daily family devotional.

■ Our family members appreciate and recognize the accomplishments of one another.

■ We are honest and open in our communication. Everyone's opinion counts.

ordless Advice

When a spouse or child has a serious problem to discuss with you, decide in advance that you will listen, nod your head occasionally, and paraphrase or ask a brief question. Otherwise, be quiet. In three out of four instances, the person in question will solve his or her own problem while talking to you. And, even if they do not solve the problem then, they will feel much better for having shared it with you. They might even thank you for the great advice you gave them . . . wordless advice.

X-traordinary Family Togetherness

Plan some family fun. Here are a few ideas to get you started. Think of more at your next family meeting.

➲ *Shine in Your Neighborhood.* Choose a family or individual in your neighborhood for whom to do a good deed. Bake some cookies, take their garbage cans out to the curb, shovel their walk, bring them a bouquet of flowers, or leave a cheery note or card in their mailbox.

➲ *Silent Cheer.* As the family sits around the dinner table, have each person talk about something he or she did particularly well that day. After each recitation, the rest of the family members will give a silent cheer. Of course, if you like noisy cheers, go for it!

➲ *Secret Buddies (Secret Santa, Secret Pal).* This activity goes by many names, but the principle is always the same—each person anonymously buys inexpensive gifts or does small acts of kindness for another family member over a short period of time.

For fifty fabulous activities to build friendships at home, see *"Nobody Likes Me": Helping Your Child Make Friends* by Elaine K. McEwan. Wheaton, IL: Harold Shaw Publishers, 1996.

Yearly Tasks

Take time to do these activities each year as a family:

◆ Evaluate your family rules.

◆ Set family goals.

◆ Give each family member an award at a special dinner.

◆ Evaluate your family's mission and vision.

Zaniness and Humor

Add a pinch of zaniness and humor to your everyday life; stir vigorously and allow to permeate the surrounding ingredients. The flavor will be subtle but definite—like the time I lost the family's underwear. Oh, the underwear really was not lost. I just could not remember where it was. Logic should have told me that the dryer was the first place to check, but I spent several days fussing about the "underwear thief" before it dawned on me where the missing unmentionables were.

I also lost the checkbook for several weeks. This was far more traumatic than the underwear episode. I looked everywhere; I was frantic. I usually kept the checkbook in a drawer in the kitchen. I never put it anywhere else unless I took it to my desk to write out the monthly bills. Where could it be? In the freezer, of course. This experience brought new meaning to the term *cold cash*. I had put the checkbook on top of the refrigerator. Then when I opened the freezer door, the checkbook had slipped behind the frozen peas. When peas were on the menu, I found the missing checkbook. What else can we do but laugh?

4

The ABCs of Keeping on Track

Organization and Time-Management Skills

There are hundreds of books on the market to help you get organized and use your time more wisely. Tantalizing titles such as *How to Have a 48-Hour Day*, *Getting Organized*, and my favorite, *How to Be Organized in Spite of Yourself*, offer the promise of personal victory over disorganization, procrastination, and the tyranny of time. But those of us with attention and learning disorders have a hard time managing complicated systems and implementing seven-step programs.

Our minds wander, we hate to be tied down to a schedule, we lose things, we break things, we forget things, we are late, we are messy, and when we finally do get around to cleaning things up we throw away our paychecks. We subscribe to dozens of magazines and rarely read any of them. We forget something every time we pack to travel. We spend enough money on organizers and daily planning systems to make a sizable dent in the national debt. Always looking for a better way, we often fail to use it when we find it.

I am not sure why I am optimistic enough to think that my advice will be any more useful than that of a thousand others, except that I do not have a comprehensive system to recommend, and I am a fellow traveler. I offer you here some relatively simple hints organized alphabetically. Each one has a key word to help you remember it, and even using just one idea could drastically improve the quality of your life. Let me offer you a "for instance."

I spent more than twenty years of my life living in a house with three floors. Consequently, nothing I ever needed was on the floor where I was located. So . . . I naturally ran (never walked, of course) up or down a flight of stairs to locate the needed scissors, ruler, tweezers, Scotch tape, or stapler. Now, it never occurred to me to take with me on this run whatever item I needed to tape or cut or measure, so . . . I naturally ran (never walked, of course) up or down another flight of stairs to resume whatever it was I was doing. That is, if I could remember what I went for, or escaped getting distracted by another task along the way, or managed to avoid falling up or down the stairs. If someone happened to be watching me (whether child or spouse), I could always count on being reminded not to run with the scissors, hammer, tweezers, or screwdriver. I would always mumble agreement, but I had no intention of changing my ways.

I cannot remember when it came to me that I could save time and energy if I just purchased several pairs of scissors and tweezers as well as multiple packages of Scotch tape and Band-Aids and stationed them at critical points about the house. It was so simple. Perhaps others had been doing this very thing for centuries, and I was just a slow learner. In any case, this one simple change in lifestyle has added years to my life. My frantic peregrinations through the house, flinging drawers open and shut while screaming to no one in particular, "Has anyone seen my scissors?" ended abruptly, and I became a much nicer person with whom to live.

I offer the following helpful hints, therefore, not to lay a guilt trip on you. Rather, they are just practical ideas that I have learned the hard way during fifty-plus years of a marvelous life that has been distracted and disorganized from time to time, but never defeated.

A rriving on Time

Try not to get a reputation for being late. I once worked with someone who lost a lot of credibility because of her chronic tardiness. She was enormously creative and terribly bright, but her colleagues often discounted her overall worth because she was always running behind. Her behavior sent the message that she did not care, was always into crisis management, and was totally out of control. I knew her better than that and could see that actually she was extremely competent and very committed and knew exactly what was happening all the time. Unfortunately, she could never really convince her boss of that.

> *Those who rush arrive first at the grave.*
>
> —*Spanish proverb*

Here are some ways I have learned over the years to conserve my time while being considerate of others:

➲ Call to confirm appointments. I cannot tell you how many times I have waited in the wrong place on the wrong day because I did not bother to confirm.

➲ If you have a service appointment (medical checkup, haircut), call to see if they are running on schedule. There is no point getting a speeding ticket only to "hurry and wait."

➲ Consider buying a cellular phone if you are chronically late. When necessary, you can notify people that you are on your way. But avoid making this a habit. It's expensive.

➲ Set the clocks in your home and car ahead. Then forget about them, if you can.

➲ Do not try to do just one more thing before you leave your home or office.

B ills

The first of the month is relentless. Your creditors do not care if you are disorganized, distracted, or dyslexic. They just want their money. I found out the hard way with my cellular phone bill. Caught in a traffic jam one day, I tried to call home only to find that my service had been disconnected. Irate, I later called the office to be told that I had not paid my bill. I was sure that I had and combed my electronic checkbook for proof. Oh, yes, I had paid the bill, but for the wrong amount—$4.59 rather than $45.90. I could just hear my mother's frequent remonstrance when I was growing up echoing in my ears, *Haste makes waste.* I did some fast talking and avoided the penalties, charges for reinstituting service, and any bad mark on my credit record. I now look at the amounts of my checks more carefully before I place them in the envelopes.

My bill-paying system generally works well for me. When a bill comes, I drop it into the bill file. Once per month, I sit down and write all of the checks, sorting the receipts and records into the appropriate files for income-tax time. It is very simple and all in one desk drawer. I have also been able to keep a well-balanced checkbook for the first time in my adult life using a computerized check-writing program. You cannot afford to be without some system for paying your bills. And I mean that literally! Late fees, interest charges, and other penalties will pile up. I have been there.

C hunking

I discovered chunking when I was in high school, and it has been a lifesaver ever since. Chunking means breaking down big jobs into small, manageable, bite-sized pieces. Here is an example of a list I made to get ready for writing a book:

> Check the on-line catalogs of local libraries
> Develop a questionnaire to send out
> Talk to editor about permission rights
> Write the introduction
> Take notes for the first chapter

D irections

Here are my cardinal rules for finding your way around the country or around the block:

■ Never trust your memory. Write things down. If you are driving alone, write directions in big block letters you can easily read while driving.

■ Do not be afraid to ask for help.

■ Install a compass in your car. This works well except when the interstate highways labeled east and west actually travel in a north-south direction.

■ If you can afford it, keep a cellular phone handy. More than once I have needed someone to talk me to a safe landing.

■ Always call ahead for directions. Then save the directions for the next time you need to travel to the same place.

E rrands

Errands are a little like death and taxes—inevitable. But if you organize them, they will be much less painful.

⊃ Include any errands that need to be run on your master list.

⊃ Establish a location in your house for collecting things that will accompany you on your errands (dry cleaning, books to be returned to the library, shoes that need repair, purchases that need to be exchanged). I have a table in the garage (I can see it from the car) where I stack these things.

⊃ "Itinerize." I arrange my errands on the list in the order I will make the stops and group them by the area in town where I will travel. I map out the route so that by the time I finish the errands and return home, I have covered the fewest miles possible.

F iles

I love to create file folders and get my life organized. The only problem is remembering the category under which I filed something important or even remembering that I created a file.

◆ Establish a file system immediately. Our lives are awash in paper, and we all need a system to deal with it. Even small children need a file system. Get them started as soon as they begin school.

◆ If more than one person will make use of the files, determine the headings together.

◆ Clean and purge your files once a year. Move yearly material that must be saved to the archives in the garage or basement. Do not keep files in your desk that you will not use regularly.

◆ File the stuff that comes across your desk. I try to do this every day, and I always insist that my secretary file things at least once a week. There is almost nothing more frustrating than digging through piles of paper looking for an important document while someone is holding on the phone. The only thing worse is losing such a document entirely.

◆ Put files that you are currently using in an easily accessible spot.

◆ Investigate visible or color-coded file systems at your local office-supply store if nothing else has worked for you.

◆ If you have children, make a file folder for each of their activities, such as soccer, piano, Scouts, church groups, etc. Then you have a place to file the packets of info and constant bombardment of paper that each of these activities generates.

◆ If you have a lot of activities, you might also consider a file system that is organized by dates. Get an expanding file marked with one through thirty-one for the days of the month. Another expander should include all the months of the year.

Go Ahead, Do It Now

This is a lesson I am still learning. I hate to hang up my clothes when I take them off. I would rather let them pile up and take care of them at the end of the week. Of course, that means bigger cleaning and pressing bills and a very messy bedroom. My behavior took a sharp turn for the better when I remarried and started living with the most disciplined and systematic man in the world. He would never dream of not hanging up his clothes or putting away his tools. He has proved to be a marvelous role model, and he never nags me when I fail in this area. I just look around and see how neat his side of the closet is, and I shape up.

Hurry

To me, *slow* has always been a four-letter word. I even have a few speeding tickets to prove it. The first words I remember hearing my parents speak to me were *slow down*. Why walk if you can run? has always been my motto. But I have paid for my fast-paced approach to life with broken dishes, bruises and abrasions, careless mistakes that cost money, and quick words that were hurtful. I wish I had known then what I know now—taking your time has its rewards.

> *Hurry is not of the Devil; it is the Devil.*
>
> —*Carl Jung*

Income Tax

While income tax is frequently the waterloo of folks with attention problems, it should not daunt you. I have done our family's taxes for more than thirty years, and I firmly believe it is not as complicated as you think it is, especially with the new computerized tax programs. Here's my simple process:

1. Keep one file labeled *income tax,* and throw everything into that file that qualifies—business-expense receipts, tax-deductible loan-interest records, investment sales, earnings stubs, etc. If the file gets too fat, split it.

2. On January 1, label as many envelopes as you need with headings (e.g., postage expenses, interest, charitable contributions). Some people use their check-writing program to keep track of these expenses, but the IRS still requires the proof provided by receipts. Sort all of the receipts into the appropriate envelopes.

3. By January 31, begin to compute your tax liability—you should have received all of the statements of earnings and interest that you need.

4. On February 15 or the nearest day off, turn on your computer if you have one; spread out your envelopes; then plug in the appropriate figures as the program walks you through the tax forms. This is the easy part. The hard part, collecting all of the stuff all year, is already done. Why pay an accountant to enter the data into a computer when you did all the hard work already?

5. If you are getting a refund, file your return immediately. If you owe money, you have two months to figure out where it will come from.

6. On February 28, scoop up all of the papers, receipts, forms, and calculator tapes, and file them in an expandable folder, box, or file crate under the appropriate year. Remember to keep these files accessible because you never know when you will get a letter from Uncle Sam asking you for further information.

J unk It

My rule of thumb is that if I have not used it for a year, I get rid of it. If you are a pack rat or are married to one, begin slowly—the process could be painful. Nevertheless, begin to reduce the clutter in your life. Clutter is distracting, it keeps you from finding what you need quickly, and it can often create anxiety. Avoid buying anything that you do not need or that you do not have a place for. Just think of how much work you will save your heirs if they do not have to dispose of your clutter after you are gone.

> *If in doubt, throw it out.*
>
> —*Anonymous*

 eys

"Where are my keys?"

—*First words of a child whose mother has ADHD*

I shared this young mother's frustration when, during one week, I locked my keys in the car while at the gas station, lost them in a snowbank at McDonald's, and misplaced them for several days when they disappeared into a pair of boots in the closet.

Here are some strategies to help you get through those "keyless" moments:

■ Retrace your steps, either mentally or physically. You will usually find them somewhere along your route.

■ Have a spare set of keys made and give them to a good friend or neighbor. Keep another set at home or in a pocket or a purse. Then, even if your keys are misplaced for a moment, you can still leave on vacation, go to a job interview, or pick up your spouse at the commuter train.

■ Tape a car key in a strategic location someplace on your automobile where it cannot be seen.

■ Identify one spot in your home, on your person, in your purse, or in a briefcase where you will always place your keys the minute you finish using them.

■ Attach something large and noisy to your keys (preferably not a child).

■ Do not share a set of keys with a spouse or child. Make another set. That way you will always have somebody to fall back on when you lose your keys.

■ If keys are your constant nemesis, consider installing keyless locks in your home and buying a car with a keyless option.

ists

I have probably made more lists in my lifetime than anyone I know. The total even includes lists to organize my lists. Now I have streamlined the lists in my life into a simple four-step process:

1. I keep one master list on my computer that contains absolutely everything I have to do without regard for importance or urgency. I add items to this list on a daily basis, organizing them into a variety of categories: correspondence, errands, writing projects, and household chores. As I add new items, I prioritize the list.

2. Each day I develop a daily list that contains everything that I hope/plan to accomplish on any given day. This list is usually written in my calendar, unless it is particularly complicated and has many steps, such as the list on my errand day when I might make as many as ten to fifteen different stops. On complicated days I use the computer and print out a list.

3. To help me keep track of things that pop into my head at odd moments, I use strategically placed notepads on the dashboard of the car (mine has a pen with a coiled plastic cord attached to it) and the bedside table. I transfer important items to my master or daily lists ASAP. Some people carry a hand-held dictating machine or personal recorder or use voice-mail at home and at work to record such reminders.

4. I have created a grocery-list template in my computer, arranged in the order of the store in which I shop. I highlight or circle the items I need, and that becomes my shopping list. I have another standardized checklist for items to pack for a trip.

M ail

Without a system for sorting your mail, you will drown in paper. I sort the mail in the garage before I enter the house. Junk mail goes straight into the trash can or recycling bin. (If you want to substantially reduce your junk mail, write to Mail Preference Service, Direct Marketing Association, 11 West 42nd St., P.O. Box 3861, New York, NY 10163-3861 and ask that your name not be sold to mailing-list companies.) Once in the house, I immediately file all bills in the bills-due file; magazines to be read go in the basket in the kitchen; mail for other family members goes in a designated spot; and correspondence that I must deal with goes in a slot on my desk. That means that all the paper you handle falls into four basic categories: TO DO/TO PAY/TO FILE/TO READ. Find a spot for each category, and your life will be much simpler.

N o . . . Learn to Say It!

Essayist Henry David Thoreau wrote in *Where I Lived and What I Lived For:*

> I practice saying no to keep my life simple, and I find

I never do it enough. It's an arduous discipline all its own, and well worth the effort.

If you have a chronic problem with saying no, try sitting in on one of the D.A.R.E. (Drug Abuse Resistance Education) classes given to kids in elementary school. The police officers who teach these classes give the kids a whole repertoire of ways to say no, and they are very effective. The next time someone asks you to do something you cannot do/do not want to do/should not do, breathe deeply and try these three things:

⊃ Remind yourself of your priorities.

⊃ Remember that no one will respect your time if you do not.

⊃ If you really think you might like to say yes, ask the person for a written job description for the job they are asking you to do. Once you have had a chance to read the specifications, you will be able to say no more vehemently.

O rganization

> "I've spent so much time getting organized and somehow I never get there."
> —*Maria Shaw, 31, conductor and performer, ADHD*

If you are organized, you will be able to find what you are looking for when you want it, get things done in a timely way, and be in control of your life.

If you cannot do these things yet, consider hiring help from a coach in getting organized.

P erfectionism

Don Aslett says in *How to Have a 48-Hour Day,*

> Expediency generally outdoes perfection.

Do it now and perfect it later.[1]

Here are some ways to conquer the perfectionism that can keep you from getting started and especially from finishing a project:

■ Resist making frequent revisions. Perfectionism is time consuming and is rarely called for.

■ Learn to challenge your assumption that in order to feel valued by others and yourself, you have to be perfect.

> *If you wait for perfect conditions, you will never get anything done.*
> —*Ecclesiastes 11:4, NLT*

■ Spend less time worrying about what others are thinking about your performance and more time concentrating on completing the job.

■ Learn to evaluate the quality of your own work so you will not be dependent on others for affirmation.

Quiet Personal Time

Find some quiet time for yourself every day. When I had small children, my quiet time was very early in the morning. I took a warm bath, did some reading, and planned my day. On some occasions, I hired a baby sitter and went to a friend's house to take a nap. When my children were in school and I was working full-time, I stopped off at the local coffee shop where I

> *Remember that time is money.*
> —*Ben Franklin*

read the paper and drew up my schedule for the day. Here are other ways to get some time for yourself:

◆ Put a sign on the door of your bedroom or office.

◆ Go to work early or stay late.

◆ Take a day off to stay at home (a vacation or personal day) or work at home on tasks that can be brought from your job.

◆ Drive your car to a peaceful spot.

◆ If you are really desperate, and can afford it, rent a hotel room or reserve a room at a retreat center. Retreat centers are often much less expensive than hotels, quieter, and more conducive to relaxation.

R outines

The more you can organize your life around routine, the less likely you will forget the really important things in life. I am currently working on including the flossing of my teeth into my bedtime routine. This goal has been difficult for me. I resist routines for the most part, preferring to "go with the flow." The term *habit-forming* has a rather pejorative meaning, but in the long run, forming good habits is essential to all of us.

S ponge Activities

In the educational world, sponge activities are things that teachers do with classes when they have just a few moments here and there, such as time waiting in line at the drinking fountain or in between class periods. Teachers aim to make the activities useful and educational and to sponge up available time. Have your own set of sponge activities for those moments when you are frustrated by waiting in the airport or at the doctor's office or at the train station or in a stadium before an event begins.

I carry my laptop with me whenever I travel. When there is an unexpected delay or layover, I get to work. I carry books and magazines with me in the car. I take correspondence with me to appointments. In waiting rooms I take the opportunity to read magazines I would never subscribe to. Whenever I use such moments to my advantage, I feel in control and less frustrated by having to wait.

Telephone Calls

Here is how you can use the telephone more effectively at work or at home:

➲ Group outgoing phone calls together.

➲ Place them in priority order.

➲ Always ask, "Is this a convenient time to talk?"

➲ Use e-mail and faxes if you can.

➲ Do other things while you are talking on the phone: fold the laundry, do your nails, clean out your wallet/purse.

➲ Always have something to do if you are put on hold. Do not sit and stare into space.

➲ Write down the name of the person who answered your call, fulfilled your request, or solved your problem. That makes for accountability and will save you hours when you have to make a call back.

➲ Take notes while talking so you can remember the important parts of the conversation.

➲ Keep a steno pad with an attached pen by each of your phones. That way, you have a written record of each call without having a lot of little pieces of paper that will get lost. Family members can use another steno pad to record notes to each other, including the note "Check phone pad in the family room!"

➲ Remember—you do not have to answer just because the phone

is ringing. For peace and quiet, turn on your answering machine and turn off the ringing. You might also consider keeping your phone number out of the directory. That will save you most of the telephone sales calls that are so disruptive to family time.

U nfinished Business

> "I'm great at starting hundreds of projects, and I'm lousy at finishing any of them."
> —*Stan Rogers, 38, trial attorney, ADHD*

We all have things that have been hanging over our heads (sometimes for years)—projects we never completed, goals we never reached. Get rid of this unfinished business in your life and move forward. Get out a big garbage can and throw these things away (both literally and figuratively). Admit that you are never going to be a size eight again and that even if you were, the clothes you are still clinging to would make you look like a page from the ancient history book. Throw away that lumber that has been rotting behind the shed. The kids are too old for a tree house anyhow. Move on. Why feel guilty every time you look at it?

Stop talking about the room you are going to remodel, and hire someone else to do the job. Start over with a fresh list that is more meaningful to where you are today. It is never too late to get your GED or go back to college. Someone I know was just ordained at the age of sixty, and she is taking her first pastorate. Grab on to a real goal and go for it.

V eracity

> "The part of ADHD that impacts my life the most is lying. I've finally, with God's help, ceased to do this, no matter what happens or what the outcome is."
> —*Rosalie Thompson, 40, florist, ADHD*

Learn to tell the truth about the things you have or have not done. People will spend a lot of time accusing you of things. You have forgotten something; you have broken something; you did not meet a deadline; you have broken a promise. 'Fess up to it and say you are sorry. Do not pretend it is not happening. Deal with it.

Worst Things First

Do the things you hate the most right away. These annoying, repetitive tasks usually do not take that much time, and you will save yourself hours of feeling guilty.

X-tras

I used to make fun of people who shopped at warehouse outlets and bought spares of everything, but I have become a convert in the last few years. Having extras of important things saves time and anguish. You do have to have some storage space, but you can always try the trunk of your car or under your bed if you are desperate. Here is a list of possible items you might stock to spare you embarrassment, frustration, time, gasoline, and money.

> *There is nothing worse than self-deception, where the deceiver is always with you.*
>
> — *Plato,* Dialogues

- ◆ Cash

- ◆ Keys

- ◆ Toilet paper

- ◆ Milk (powdered is especially handy)

- ◆ Paper towels

- ◆ Pantyhose

- ◆ Personal products

- ◆ Diapers

- ◆ Pens/pencils

- ◆ Film

Yearly Jobs

There are several jobs that you ought to do at least once yearly to maintain a modicum of organization in your life:

- ■ Clean out your files.

- ■ Clean out your closets.

- ■ Give stuff to the Goodwill, the Salvation Army, a veterans group, a homeless or abused women's shelter, or any other charity.

- ■ Put your income-tax stuff into storage.

- ■ Set some meaningful and realistic goals for the next year. If you only set one goal and accomplish it, be proud.

- ■ Give all of the canned goods in your pantry that you have not used in the past year to the local food bank.

- ■ Cancel all the magazine, book club, and CD/tape club subscriptions for items that you have not read or listened to in the last six months.

- ■ Throw away all of the newspapers and magazines you have not read. The news is outdated, and you will find the same articles under different titles in forthcoming magazines and newspapers.

- ■ Update your address book, card file, or computer directory.

Z aniness

New Zealand-born author Katherine Mansfield writes,

> When we can begin to take our failures nonseriously, it means we are ceasing to be afraid of them. It is of immense importance to learn to laugh at ourselves.[2]

Humor is an essential part of my life. When you are impulsive, hyperactive, and distractible, life gets pretty funny sometimes. A few years ago, I rushed home from work, frantic to wrap a package and get it in the mail before the post office closed. I tore off my office duds and hastily pulled on a pair of slacks from the dryer (the place where I often stored clothing I was not wearing). I breathlessly arrived at the post office in time. I took my place in line and waited patiently. As the line moved forward, someone tapped on my shoulder. A woman tentatively inquired, "Are those yours?" She was pointing at a pair of women's panties lying at my feet. I had two choices at this point: leave a perfectly good pair of my underwear on the floor of the post office, or claim my belonging (static cling and all). I chose the latter and tried to gracefully and surreptitiously retrieve the lacy undies and stuff them in my purse. I resolved to never again leave my clothing "stored" in the dryer. The best part, though, is the delight I have had in telling this story on myself ever since that moment of embarrassment.

5

The ABCs of Working

Getting a Job and Keeping It

Work is important to me. It always has been. I started doing it when I was six years old, and I am still at it. I have been blessed in my life always to have work that has consumed me, work that has matched my gifts and talents, and purposeful work that has helped and enriched the lives of others. I hope that you can find meaningful and exciting work to make your life complete.

A ccommodations

Accommodations are changes in the workplace environment that employers must make for individuals with documented disabilities. They include, but are not limited to,

◆ access to computers with spell checkers

◆ access to tape recorders to take notes and to record instructions from supervisors

◆ access to calculators to speed up calculations

◆ written directions for work to be performed

◆ models of performance or samples of work

◆ permission to take more time to accomplish tasks even if it means working overtime

◆ access to a quiet office with a minimum of distractions

◆ frequent feedback and performance appraisals

◆ more structure and immediate deadlines

◆ direction given by only one person

B oredom

If working from nine to five will make you crazy with boredom, there are many ways of structuring the work week that offer more flexibility and variety, important needs for those of us with attention and learning disorders. Try one of these possibilities if you are in a rut: temping, contract employment, job sharing, working at home, a compressed work week, flextime, self-employment, and permanent part-time work.

Breaking Out of 9 to 5 by Maria Laqueur and Donna Dickinson. Princeton: Peterson's, 1994.

C reativity

> "At work [private law practice] I've surrounded myself with staff members who are good at details and completing my projects, because by the time a project is half over, I've moved on to something new."
> —*Stan Rogers, 38, trial attorney, ADHD*

If you are a highly creative individual but you are not presently tapping this potential through your career or extracurricular activities, you are no doubt miserable. If you are not regularly experiencing the *flow* described by psychologist Mihaly Csikszentmihalyi,[1] you are missing out on one of life's great joys. Flow is something that occurs when you are engrossed in a project of your choosing rather than meeting someone else's expectations. Individuals with learning and attention disorders are often very creative and intuitive. Their tolerance for ambiguity, their dogged determination, and their wacky ways of making the familiar strange often drive the linear, left-brained types right up the wall. Here are some ways to tap into your creative side while continuing to function in a world that values steadiness, reliability, and predictability:

■ Make sure you have people around, over, or under you who can keep the plates spinning or the balls in the air after you have started the performance.

■ Be the creative genius in your own or a family business where being fired for your flights of fancy is unlikely. Just make sure that another family or organization member is willing and able to handle the details and follow-through.

■ If you need structure and high expectations in your work life, explore your creative possibilities through moonlighting or a hobby.

■ Enter contests, sell your work, join a writing or painting group, or start your own business on the side.

D aily Planners

Figuring out how to use your calendar or daily planner is essential to coping with attention and learning difficulties. You will probably buy and discard many of them before you find the right one for you. Here are my guidelines for calendar usage:

➲ Your calendar has to be manageable enough in size so that you can take it with you everywhere—church, shopping, the office, out for dinner. There is nothing more frustrating than to have to call people back because they do not have their calendars.

➲ Your planner has to contain your entire life. Do not have one calendar for work and another for home.

➲ Write down all of your standing appointments and deadlines in your calendar even if you think you will remember them.

➲ Review calendars with your secretary, spouse, or older children on a weekly basis (at least) so that kids get picked up at the sitter's and you do not schedule a major project on your secretary's vacation day.

➲ Keep your yearly calendars in a storage box or area so that you can gain access to them quickly. I constantly refer to my old calendars for pertinent information.

➲ Always write down the phone number, address, and directions for any appointments that will take you to new territory.

➲ Make sure there are some blank pages for keeping notes and making lists.

➲ Do not be reluctant to toss out your expensive planning system if it is not working for you.

E ntrepreneurs

Folks with attention and learning disorders are often natural entrepreneurs. An article in the *Archives of General Psychiatry*[2] compared a group of ninety-one men who had been diagnosed with ADD in childhood with a control group of ninety-five men. The most interesting bit of data to emerge from this study, in my opinion, was that 20 percent of the group with ADD grew up to own their own companies whereas only 5 percent of the control group ended up "out on their own." Running a business is perfect for the person who wants to run the show without anwering to anyone but him or herself.

Focus Your Energy by Thom Hartmann. New York: Pocket Books, 1994.

F eedback

Learning how to accept constructive criticism is a difficult but crucial skill for success in relationships, whether in our personal lives or in the workplace. *Defensive* was the best word to describe me for much of my life. I wanted to be perfect, and when somebody close to me thought I was not perfect, I found reasons to argue the point. I worked overtime, making sure that I could not be faulted, afraid of being discovered as less than perfect. Conversely, I could always diagnose in clinical detail exactly what was wrong with anyone or anything I encountered. Although I may not have been willing to confront offenders with their transgressions, I could certainly be counted on to detail them for others. In my immaturity and naïveté I believed that this approach to life was productive. Fortunately, I grew up along the way (with a little help from my friends).

As you work on accepting feedback (constructive or otherwise) from employers and others, avoid these behaviors:

◆ Arguing, interrupting, or shouting at your boss

◆ Not looking at your boss

◆ Walking away from your boss while he or she is still talking to you

◆ Making a joke or humorous remark

◆ Claiming you do not understand

◆ Complaining about working conditions

◆ Acting helpless

◆ Blaming your boss's style

◆ Saying the boss is prejudiced

◆ Blabbing everything to coworkers after your meeting with the boss

◆ Acting like a martyr

◆ Overreacting to criticism for the smallest things

G oals

Peter Drucker writes in *Adventures of a Bystander,* "Whenever anything is accomplished, it is being done, I have learned, by a monomaniac with a mission."[3]

If you are not in the habit of setting professional and/or career goals for yourself, you may be of all people most miserable. You long for accomplishment and completion and envy those who "just do it." To avoid that, set daily short-term goals, monthly to quarterly midrange goals, and yearly long-term goals. Write them down; commit to them. Share them with friends and family members who can help you reach them.

> *If we do not know what port we're steering for, no wind is favorable.*
>
> —*Seneca*

H ooper's Law

Grace Hooper, former rear admiral of the U.S. Navy, is said to have coined this phrase: *Beg forgiveness rather than asking permission.* This insight is truly a way of life for those of us with attention and learning disorders. Because of our impulsivity, energy, and creativity, we frequently launch into projects without going through appropriate channels. Because we sometimes misunderstand or do not hear the directions properly, we bumble on ahead, mindless of the havoc we are about to create. Or, we just know that no one could possibly object to the marvel of what we are about to do. Besides, it would take too long to get permission. Two caveats: You can only fall back on Admiral Hooper's law once in a while, and your marvelous idea better make a lot of money and not get anyone in trouble.

I nterruptions

Folks with attention and learning disorders thrive on interruptions even when they keep us from accomplishing our tasks. After all, if we are being interrupted, we have an excuse for not doing what we did not want to do anyhow. Interruptions keep us from being bored, frustrated, or anxious. Many people actually get upset when they are interrupted. I generally welcome interruptions. I race to answer the telephone, wait eagerly for the mail to arrive, and love unexpected visitors. Here are some ways to minimize interruptions if you are serious about dealing with the problem:

➲ Avoid eye contact with people by facing your desk away from the door or blocking your visibility with a large plant or partition.

➲ Minimize nonessential interruptions by scheduling them for other times of day.

➲ Jot down a note about what you were doing when you were interrupted.

➲ Keep a pad of paper handy and jot down anything that intrudes on your thoughts. That might include items you need to pick up at the store on the way home or something you forgot to tell someone. Handle those things when you take a break from your more concentrated work.

➲ Pay attention to your most productive times of day. For many people, that is the morning. Protect those highly productive times from interruptions and try to do your most demanding work then.

J ob Search

Here are some strategies to help you as you begin any new job search:

Learn all about your prospective field. Schedule some informational interviews with people you know in the field you wish to enter. An informational interview is something I often recommend to new graduates who are looking for jobs. Here is how it works:

1. Identify an organization, industry, or individual for whom you would like to work (a branch manager of a local real estate company, an elementary school principal, the local manufacturing company).

2. Call the individual and ask if he or she would give you thirty minutes to help you make some decisions about where you would like to work.

3. Develop a list of questions that you would like to have answered. Some possibilities might include: What are the most important skills you are looking for in people you are hiring now? Do you have any recommendations for training that might be helpful for someone wanting to work in this field? What are the most challenging problems your business will be facing in the next decade?

4. Conduct the interview. Make sure you limit it to the specified time, and be sure to send the person you interviewed a gracious thank-you note.

Invest in your appearance. Update your haircut and buy one great-looking interview suit or outfit. There is nothing more devastating to your self-confidence than feeling shabby. And your appearance deserves an investment of time and money.

Take a class. Go to a local community college if you are not up to date on technology. The world of computers, data-base management, e-mail, and office productivity has grown explosively in the last ten years, and few workplaces have escaped the impact. Most jobs today require some sophistication in the world of computers.

Update your letters of reference. If you have not worked recently, ask the people for whom you have done volunteer work to write recommendations. They will be more timely and reflect your current level of expertise.

Seek out career counseling and testing. Many community colleges offer career counseling and testing that is free to residents. You can also check your telephone directory for private firms that provide aptitude testing.

Make use of the resources available for specific types of job hunters. For women who are entering the work force for the first time, write to the Educational Testing Service (Publication Order Services, CN 6736, Princeton, NJ 08541-6736) and ask for the following inexpensive books, all by Ruth B. Ekstrom:

- HAVE SKILLS Women's Workbook—Finding Jobs Using Your Homemaking and Volunteer Work Experience, How to Get College Credit for What You Have Learned as a Homemaker and Volunteer

- HAVE SKILLS Employer's Guide—Matching Women and Jobs

- HAVE SKILLS Counselor's Guide—Helping Women Find Jobs Using Their Homemaking and Volunteer Work Experience.

For people with disabilities, check out these resources:

- "Job Hunting Tips for the So-Called Handicapped or People Who Have Disabilities." A Supplement to *What Color Is Your Parachute?* 1991 (available from Ten Speed Press, Box 7123, Berkeley, CA 94707).

- The Job Accommodation Network, 809 Allen Hall, Box 6123 West Virginia University, Morgantown, WV 26505-6123, 800-526-7234. This is an information and consulting network that serves people with disabilities and their employers in the U.S. and Canada by assisting with job-accommodation recommendations.

Buy a copy of *What Color Is Your Parachute?* by Richard N. Bolles

(Ten Speed Press, Box 7123, Berkeley, CA 94707). This is a fabulous book that every job hunter should read from cover to cover.

Keep things in perspective. Remember that there is not one best kind of job for individuals with attention and learning disorders. Some of us find we need jobs with freedom and autonomy, while others crave structure from a job since that aspect is lacking in our lives. The important thing is finding a job that fits well with your profile and needs. That might take some time, but do not be discouraged.

K now Thyself

Know your strengths and weaknesses. If you can afford the outlay, find a career-planning and placement organization that can administer a battery of aptitude, interest, and personality tests to you if they are not available from your community college. These tests will provide you with a better understanding of your talents, and a skilled counselor can make recommendations about the types of jobs in which individuals with your profile have found success.

L istening

This skill is as important in the workplace as it is in the family setting. Effective listening has three steps—preparation, focusing, and responding. Since I am hearing impaired, I have little room for any margin of error when I listen to others. I have to be doubly disciplined when attending business meetings. The same strategies that work for me will help you be a better listener. Let me illustrate:

⊃ *Prepare.* When someone catches me off guard with a verbal interruption, I usually have no clue about what was said. My mind was elsewhere; I was not tuned in. In business and professional settings, I must choose ahead of time to stay constantly focused, always anticipating what might be discussed and where the conversation might be going.

⊃ *Focus.* I try to choose my surroundings (quiet rooms or offices with closed doors) and arrange my physical position (to the left of the speaker in a one-on-one conversation or at the front in a large-group setting) to maximize what I will hear.

⊃ *Respond.* I show the speaker or individual with whom I am conversing that I am tuned in to what he or she is saying. I try not to let my eyes or ears wander. Occasionally I nod my head, smile, or murmur a phrase of agreement. I have also learned to ask questions early in the conversation if I have missed an important point. Losing track of a conversation can be very embarrassing, I have discovered.

M entors

Find a mentor from whom you can learn and receive coaching. Your mentor could be someone in your own workplace or someone in a related field who works somewhere else. You may find it difficult to see yourself and your work situation objectively, and a good mentor is worth his or her weight in gold.

N etworking

Networking is connecting with people for the purpose of advancing your career. You may be ambivalent about this concept, feeling reticent about imposing yourself on someone you scarcely know. But if you consider networking as relationship building, rather than "looking for favors," you may be surprised at how it can enrich your life, both personally and professionally. Try these simple networking hints:

■ Acknowledge people you know. When you read about one of them in the newspaper, clip the article and send it with a congratulatory note.

■ Write thank-you notes to people with whom you work—people who would not expect to receive a note from you, such as subordinates or coworkers.

■ Identify someone whom you admire for what he or she has accomplished in his or her professional life. Invite that individual to lunch or breakfast and solicit advice about your career goals.

■ Stay in touch with people with whom you have worked in past jobs.

■ Take a class to enhance your skills (computers, team planning, any advanced skill needed in your job), and get to know all the people in the class. Stay after class and get to know the professor.

O bstacles to Success

Sometimes those of us with attention and learning disorders are our own worst enemies in the workplace. Are you guilty of any of these no-nos?

◆ overstepping the bounds and getting into other people's jobs

◆ letting the boring, tedious stuff go while you have fun with a new project

◆ saying yes to more than you should

◆ stirring up conflict

◆ talking too much so other people cannot finish their work

◆ leaving overly long voice-mail messages

◆ asking questions that go on longer than the answer

◆ telling anecdotes that never end or have no point

♦ asking your boss the same questions over and over

♦ being unwilling to "pay your dues"

♦ telling your boss how to do his or her job

P ossibilities to Consider in Your Future

The research data is scary on how many different jobs an individual starting a career today will have before retirement. And even that picture is changing almost yearly. The good news is that those of us with attention and learning disorders are ready-made for this constantly changing employment scene. We are flexible and can shift gears at a moment's notice. Here are some of the new ways to consider employment in the twenty-first century:

⊃ Downshifters jump off the fast track to reduce stress and strike a balance between work and personal interests.

⊃ Re-careerers repeatedly update and acquire new skills to stay marketable and to give themselves the flexibility to change careers if they want to or are forced to.

⊃ Plateauers intentionally put their careers on hold by turning down promotions in favor of devoting time and energy to other activities.

⊃ Portfolio people develop an array or portfolio of skills that allow them to move easily among a variety of assignments or jobs.

⊃ Casserole careerers juggle many part-time jobs at once in lieu of one full-time job, either to make ends meet or to build new skills for a subsequent career.

⊃ Career shifters, career changers, or career switchers reduce stress or replace a lost job by applying their skills and experience to a new job in a related field or to the same job in a less stressful field.[4]

Question Your Values

If you are thinking about quitting your present job because you do not like it, take a few minutes and reflect on what you value in a job before you look for a new position. Armed with this information, you will be a more informed and effective job hunter. Look at the lists below. For each set (A, B, C), select the value that is most important to you:

SET A

Action—being employed in an environment where decisions need to be made quickly and frequently

Creativity—discovering new and innovative ways of doing things as a usual everyday pattern

Precision—working in an atmosphere that allows little room for error

Stability—performing tasks that are similar from day to day

Set A, most important:_____

SET B

Mental challenge—engaging in work that requires considerable analyzing and abstract thinking

Physical challenge—accomplishing tasks that require physical strength and stamina

Location—working in surroundings that allow me to pursue the leisure activities I enjoy most

Moral fulfillment—promoting and advancing the moral standards I feel are important

Set B, most important:_____

SET C

Competition—working in an environment in which my results are constantly pitted against those of my peers

Cohesiveness—working as a member of a team that is highly interdependent

Independence—having little contact with people; working alone

Power—having authority over and responsibility for the work of others

Set C, most important:_____

My current job satisfies . . .
a. all three I selected
b. two I selected
c. only one I selected
d. none of those I selected[5]

R ésumés

You can buy books, take classes, rent videos, or hire a consultant to help you write your résumé. There are dozens of people waiting to take your money. Before you sign on the dotted line, try these helpful hints:

◆ Tailor your résumé to the type of job you are seeking. Do not develop a "one size fits all" résumé.

◆ Keep your résumé to one page in length.

◆ Describe your accomplishments with action verbs.

◆ Ask someone you know and trust to give you feedback on the appearance and content of your résumé.

◆ Proofread your résumé at least five times and on different days.

◆ Spend money on printing and paper. Do not be clever or cute.

◆ Be sure to get permission from references before including their names.

S urvival Strategies for the Workplace

These strategies work for me. Add yours to the list.

■ Get up and move around frequently. When I fail to do this, I make mistakes, and I am less effective.

■ Pace yourself. You do not have to do it all at once.

■ Schedule intensive work in time-limited chunks.

■ Carry your calendar with you at all times. It was this strategy that made me decide to get rid of my cumbersome notebook planner and start carrying a very small pocket version.

■ Wear a watch with an alarm so you avoid losing track of important appointments.

■ Do not volunteer to do everything that needs to be done.

■ Do not take a job with more than one boss. This was one of the reasons I rejected the school superintendency as a viable option for me. I did not want to work for seven bosses.

■ Write it down. One colleague I worked with jotted notes on the inside of his hand. Paper is preferable, though, and definitely more professional.

■ Take time-outs if you feel yourself reaching a breaking point.

■ Use relaxation techniques in your job. Close the door and do some deep breathing.

■ Plan and prioritize before jumping in. Think before acting.

■ Take notes at meetings and during important phone calls (especially those times when you will be held accountable for some action).

■ Obtain and distribute minutes of important meetings. If you have a meeting and a decision is reached, keeping a written record of what happened will lessen the chances for confusion.

T ime-Out

Take a time-out when confronted with feedback or criticism to deal with your feelings of anger and frustration. When you feel yourself beginning to boil over, count to ten, go to the rest room, or scribble your feelings on a sheet of paper.

> *Learn to disagree without being disagreeable.*
>
> —H. Jackson Browne

U rgency Addiction

> "Everything is equal to me; I have an urgency addiction."
>
> —*Maria Shaw, 31, conductor and performer, ADHD*

All goals were not created equal. Some things are important and urgent. Get those done right away. Some things are important but not urgent. Accomplishing those things is what separates effective individuals from ineffective ones. Some goals are urgent but not important. Most of us let far too many of those dominate our lives. Be able to label the category in which you are working, and make plans to shift your emphasis more frequently to the important but not urgent category. In his thought-provoking discussion on how time can keep you prisoner, Ralph Keyes suggests the following guidelines:

◌ Reflect regularly on your life as a whole (composing and reviewing your own obituary is one way to do this).

◌ Evaluate all activities, even the

> *The essence of living is choosing. And, having chosen what really matters most to us, ruthlessly giving up the rest.*
>
> —*Ralph Keyes*

most trivial, by whether they add to that life.

⊃ Remember the lesson of brush-with-death survivors—each day could be our last, but the day can never be enjoyed if we are too rushed.

⊃ Weed out ruthlessly whatever does not enhance your day—tasks, errands, TV shows, people.

⊃ Ask yourself repeatedly, *Does what I'm doing contribute to the life I want to lead?*[6]

First Things First : To Live, To Love, To Learn, To Leave a Legacy by Stephen Covey, A. Roger Merrill, and Rebecca Merrill. New York: Simon & Schuster, 1994.

V erve

This is a quality that folks with attention and learning disorders have in abundance. Their enthusiasm, fervor, liveliness, and imagination can often be overwhelming to others who approach life with a more easygoing approach. Be careful to use restraint when beginning a new position. In my younger days I was hired as a learning-center teacher to replace someone who was retiring. Eager to clean house and rearrange the center to meet my specifications, I borrowed a key to the school from one of the teachers I knew. In my naiveté, I did not consider the inappropriateness of a new teacher dismantling the long-term work of the teacher she'd replaced. I was a woman with a mission. Fortunately, my principal was a person of great understanding and understatement. "Well," he said as he viewed what wonders I had wrought in a single weekend, "you certainly didn't waste any time putting your stamp on this library." I have since learned to temper my enthusiasm with more common sense.

Work Styles

Understanding your work style can help you function more efficiently, particularly if you must work closely with others. If your work style does not match that of your team members, or if your secretary does not understand how you function best and is constantly trying to change you, there's a chance of trouble ahead. Do you recognize your style in any of these somewhat annoying profiles?

■ Ms. Hopper jumps from one project to another and rarely completes anything from start to finish.

■ Dr. Perfectionist Plus is never quite satisfied with the results of his/her efforts. Projects are rarely completed on time because there is just one more thing to redo.

■ Mrs. Allergic to Detail is great on formulating big plans and projects, but she is weak on the follow-through necessary to make something happen.

■ Mr. Fence Sitter leaves everything to chance because he has trouble making decisions. Decision by default is the rule of the day.

■ Miss Cliffhanger thrives on excitement, last-minute delays, and management by crisis.

■ Ms. Everything Out works with everything she needs right in front of her. Her files, cabinets, and drawers are empty.

■ Mr. Nothing Out cannot stand clutter and confuses neatness with organization.

■ Dr. Pack Rat saves everything, including magazines from the '60s.[7]

X -pert

Carve out a niche for yourself wherever you work. Become particularly adept at something you do and make yourself indispensable. This expertise will make your boss and coworkers more amenable to forgiving you when you are forgetful, outspoken, self-centered, irresponsible, or just plain weird. If you have no expert knowledge and are also forgetful, outspoken, etc., you will be the first to go when your boss needs to fire somebody. Find your place to shine!

> *Work is not primarily a thing one does to live, but the thing one lives to do.*
>
> —Dorothy Sayers

Y easty

This is a fascinating word with many worderful synonyms: excited, impassioned, steamed up, keyed up, hopped up, turned on, effervescent, and carried away. Do any of these adjectives describe your approach to a job that you love? Find a job and employer that appreciates your enthusiasm and creativity.

Z ippity Doo Dah

Kahlil Gibran wrote in *The Prophet*,[8]

> Work is Love made visible. And if you can't work with love but only with distaste, it is better that you should leave your work and sit at the gate of the temple and take alms of the people who work with joy.

Do all you can to find work that you can love, work that gives you satisfaction, work that has purpose.

6

The ABCs of Lifelong Learning

Going Back to School

"I repeated the fourth grade. In high school I couldn't pass a test, especially in U.S. history. I've had a lot of depression, always wishing I could be like others."

—*Eleanor Duncan, 73, widowed missionary, LD*

"I was always dumb. I was always behind everyone in class. I felt stupid. I hated school so much. I never fit in anywhere."

—*Phyllis Cameron, 50, unemployed widow, LD*

"I never felt I could measure up to what was expected of me. I always tried to please my teachers, but school was so hard for me."

—*Rosalie Thompson, 40, florist, ADHD*

People with attention and learning disorders have some of the most devastating experiences of their lives in school settings. Some turn into the class clown in an attempt to cover up academic deficits.

Others endure the teasing of peers, the nagging of teachers and parents, and the loneliness of defeat. A large percentage just plain quit as soon as they can. So if the thought of returning to the classroom leaves you with palpitations and sweaty palms, you are not alone.

There is hope, however. Hundreds of individuals are deciding to give it another try. Colleges and universities are opening their doors to students with attention and learning disorders, providing special programs, accommodations in the classroom, counselors, and tutors. Literacy programs are available for those who do not know how to read. You have a lot going for you now that you did not have back in your school days—your maturity, your desire, and the resources of an educational community that has realized that even one mind is too precious a thing to waste.

Take the first step today and discover that learning can be fun!

Auditory Learning

Compare yourself to the following list of descriptors to see if you are an auditory learner. If so, then use the tips that follow to help you become a more effective learner. Play to your strengths rather than bemoaning your weaknesses.

◆ You need to hear it to know it.

◆ You have trouble with reading and writing.

◆ You have trouble following written instructions.

◆ You have a difficult time figuring out what people are thinking from their body language and facial expressions.

◆ You process things you see very slowly.

◆ You are easily distracted by visual stimuli.

Tips for Auditory Learners

1. Use books on tape rather than reading textbooks (see *Books on Tape).*

2. Tape class lectures and listen to them while driving or exercising.

3. Sign up for classes in which you will be tested more on the material you hear in class rather than on readings in the textbook.

4. Vocalize written information to remember it.

5. Translate pictures into spoken words as you study.

6. Arrange for test-taking modifications, such as having questions and directions read aloud or put on tape.

7. Join a study group where the material to be learned is discussed.

Books on Tape

> "I send in two copies of each of my textbooks to the State Services Recording for the Blind and get a cassette tape back that I can use for studying."
> —*Teresa Lorenzen, 34, college student and mother, LD*

If you have a diagnosed and documented attention and/or learning disorder, you are eligible to have your college textbooks recorded on cassette tapes. You may benefit from contacting either or both of the following services to determine your eligibility:

Recording for the Blind
20 Roszel Road
Princeton, NJ 08540
609-452-0606
RFB records educational textbooks for those individuals with learning disabilities who meet eligibility requirements.

Services for the Blind and Physically Handicapped
Library of Congress

1291 Taylor Street NW
Washington, DC 20542
800-424-8567
202-707-5100

The Library of Congress provides recordings of current books and magazines for individuals whose disability prevents the use of printed material. Applicants must have a documented disability to receive this service.

C ollege Courses

Do your homework before signing up for classes:

➲ Choose courses that interest you. Do not sign up for something if deep down you know you will cut class.

➲ Choose professors that match your learning style. If you have good auditory memory, choose lecture classes. If you have good visual memory, find classes that rely on textbooks.

➲ Do not take more than one difficult course per quarter or semester.

➲ Do not take more than three courses per quarter or semester.

D emand Your Rights

Do not be shy about taking advantage of every bit of help you have coming to you. Your goal is to learn; do not let anything stand in your way. Be assertive. Seek out a counselor or advocate at the college you attend. Find the Special Services office and make an appointment. Seek out other students who have succeeded in spite of their attention or learning disorders. Ask them for advice and assistance. See X-ercise Your Rights for a list of common adjustments that can be made for students with special needs.

Everything You Need to Know to Be a Success in School

There are no secrets to success in the academic world. All of the secrets have been told in the hundreds of available books and guides about study skills. Here are the skills that are most crucial, in my opinion. Find a book or a person who can teach you the skills you lack. You need to know

- how to read and remember new material in your textbooks

- how to keep track of homework assignments

- how to write a research paper

- how to survey a new textbook

- how to write an essay

- how to use the library

> *Begin at the beginning," the King said gravely, "and go till you come to the end; then stop.*
>
> —*Lewis Carroll*

Effective Study Skills by James K. Semones. Fort Worth, TX: Harcourt Brace Jovanovich, 1991.

Finding Favor

There are certain behaviors that impress and get the attention of any teacher. Trust me. I have been on both sides of the blackboard. Try these tricks to connect early in the semester with your professors:

◆ Arrive early and sit in the front. Maintain eye contact with the professor.

◆ Maintain a listening posture and attitude. Sit forward in your chair. Nod. Smile.

◆ Demonstrate through your behavior that you are interested in what is being said and in doing well in the class.

Graphic (or Cognitive) Organizers

If you are a visual learner, use graphic organizers to help you study. Graphic organizers are visual aids, diagrams, and drawings that help you pattern your thinking in logical ways. Check out these resources for a more complete discussion of graphic organizers.

Solving School Problems by Elaine K. McEwan. Wheaton, IL: Harold Shaw Publishers, 1992.

Seven Ways of Knowing: Teaching for Multiple Intelligences by David Lazear. Palatine, IL: IRI/Skylight Publishing, 1994.

> *We have all forgot more than we remember.*
>
> —*Thomas Fuller, 1732*

Hemisphericity

Another way of looking at how people think and learn is hemisphericity. With the discovery that the brain is divided into two sections, or hemispheres, researchers became aware that certain behaviors and ways of thinking seemed to be centered more in one hemisphere than the other. Many of us show a definite preference for either the right or the left side; thus the labels right-brained and left-brained. Of course, the brain is truly more subtle and complex than these oversimplified descriptions allow. But even these generalizations offer helpful insights.

Distinctly *right-brained* individuals make better artists and performers. Distinctly *left-brained* people do better as accountants and chemists. We survived for centuries without knowing about hemisphericity, but an understanding of which thinking or reasoning patterns (learning styles) characterize each hemisphere, along with the related school skills, can be helpful as you understand how to compensate for your attention and learning disorders.

⊃ Primarily left-brained individuals do their thinking and reasoning in an analytical-sequential fashion. They prefer verbal explanations, use language to remember, produce ideas logically, like structured experiences, and approach problems seriously.[1]

⊃ Individuals who are primarily right-brained do their processing in a wholistic-simultaneous way. They prefer visual explanations, use images to remember, produce ideas intuitively, prefer abstract thinking tasks, like open, fluid experiences, and approach problems playfully.[2]

You may already have figured out that right-brained individuals are at a distinct disadvantage in school settings that emphasize symbols, language, phonics, talking, and reciting. If you are right-brained you need lots of hands-on, experiential learning. Your challenge as a right-brained learner is to find teachers and learning opportunities that match your style.

I ntelligence

Do not get hung up on feeling dumb. There are many kinds of intelligence. IQ tests do not measure imagination or creativity. They cannot begin to describe the power of motivation and desire. Your IQ score says nothing about your athletic, musical, or artistic abilities. Thomas Armstrong does a terrific job of describing "seven kinds of smart."[3] See how many describe you.

Verbal/Linguistic Intelligence. We exhibit this kind of intelligence when we speak to each other and put our thoughts down on paper. Storytelling, humor that involves plays on words, metaphors, similes, and the use of proper grammar when writing or speaking are all aspects of this kind of intelligence.

Logical/Mathematical Intelligence. This intelligence is exhibited when dealing with a situation that requires problem solving or meeting a new challenge. Scientific thinking, the ability to see abstract patterns, and the ability to recognize relationships between separate and distinct pieces of information are characteristics of logical/mathematical intelligence.

Visual/Spatial Intelligence. This intelligence is shown through the ability to visualize things such as furniture in a room or an architectural drawing. If you are able to read maps and get to places easily, you have strong visual/spatial intelligence. Artists abound with this intelligence.

Bodily/Kinesthetic Intelligence. This intelligence is demonstrated through all of the physical abilities as well as the memory of how to do certain things such as type, ride a bike, park a car, and play a sport.

Musical/Rhythmic Intelligence. Those who are able to maintain rhythm, feel a musical beat, and develop rhythmic patterns through writing music have this type of intelligence.

Interpersonal Intelligence. If you delight in being part of a team effort, are skilled in both verbal and nonverbal communication, and are able to read the moods, temperaments, and intentions of others, you have interpersonal intelligence.

Intrapersonal Intelligence. Individuals with strong intrapersonal intelligence are exceptionally gifted in understanding themselves. They are self-reflective and enjoy spending time alone with themselves.

Seven Pathways of Learning: Teaching Students and Parents about Multiple Intelligences by David Lazear. Tucson, AZ: Zephyr Press, 1994.
Multiple Intelligences: The Theory in Practice by Howard Gardner. New York: Basic Books, 1993.

J oy of Learning

Many adults with attention and learning disorders had disastrous experiences in elementary, junior high, or high school. They remember embarrassment, frustration, and distrust of teachers and learning. If you are among them, do not be afraid to reclaim the joy of learning you had as a very small child. Your maturity, advancements in learning technology, and the help that is available if you have a documented disability will open up new vistas for you.

K inesthetic/Tactile Learning

Compare yourself to the following list of descriptors to see if you are a kinesthetic/tactile learner. If so, then use the following numbered list to help you become a more effective learner. Play to your strengths.

- You have an excellent sense of direction.

- You enjoy experiential, hands-on learning.

- You have a hard time sitting still.

- You would rather plunge into something and figure out the directions as you go.

- You are well coordinated in sports and physical activities and can easily remember dance, gymnastic, and sports movements.

- You can only know something after you have done it or experienced it.

- You would rather learn by watching someone else do something than by reading about it or hearing someone describe it.

Tips for Kinesthetic/Tactile Learners

1. Take frequent "movement" breaks between study periods.

2. Use computer-assisted instruction to build in a strong experiential component.

3. Enroll in classes/curricula that emphasize hands-on learning (laboratories, performance-based learning, apprentice-ships and internships, model making, role-playing, and group work).

4. Memorize or drill while walking or exercising.

5. Trace letters and words to learn spelling and help remember facts.

L istening

Listening to lectures and discussions in classrooms is hard work. Perhaps you have never thought of it as work; after all, you are just sitting there. But your passivity and lack of involvement may be the big reason why you do not remember and have difficulty learning. Be intentional about your listening.

⊃ Get ready to listen before you come to class by reading the assignment, reviewing the syllabus, and jotting down any questions you may need to have answered during the lecture and discussion.

⊃ Sit in the front of the room so that nothing can interfere with your concentration and eye contact with the teacher.

⊃ Even if you have someone taking class notes for you, listen carefully and coach the note taker about when to underline key concepts.

⊃ Use colored pens or highlighters to emphasize important ideas or potential exam questions.

⊃ Put question marks in the margin of your notebook paper to indicate that you do not understand something. Stay after class and ask the teacher to explain.

Memory Strategies

Acquire and perfect as many different strategies as possible to help you remember things. Remembering, along with understanding, is the basis for learning. Even if you do not have what you consider a good memory, there are dozens of ways to compensate. I should know—I have used all of them with great success. I have also taught them to kids as an elementary school teacher and principal. Experiment with a variety of approaches and find out what works for you.

◆ You have got to understand in order to remember. Avoid rote memorization and attach meaning to what you want to remember.

◆ Be intentional about remembering things. You cannot afford to be relaxed and laissez-faire. You must work at it.

◆ Associate a new piece of information with something you already know. Organize and categorize new information as you would put away groceries after shopping.

◆ Chunk large blocks of information into smaller cohesive pieces and remember them as units.

◆ If you are poetic, make up a rhyme or silly sentence.

◆ Use a visual aid (see *Graphic Organizers*). Pictures, charts, mind maps, and time lines can all help to fix important ideas in our minds.

◆ Intentionally use all of your senses when you are trying to memorize and learn something new. Write it down; say it aloud; draw a picture of it.

◆ Invent a mnemonic device, a word that is spelled using the first letters of several key words to help you remember a list of ideas or concepts.

◆ Associate what you want to remember with something slightly offbeat or wacky.

◆ Before you make all the effort to memorize something, make sure it is important. Do not try to remember everything.

◆ Make up a story that will help chain or link the ideas you want to remember.

The Memory Book by Harry Lorayne and Jerry Lucas. New York: Ballantine Books, 1974.

Use Both Sides of Your Brain by Tony Buzan. New York: Penguin Books, 1989.

Note Taking

Whether you are taking notes for yourself or you have someone else taking them for you, be sure to follow these simple rules:

■ Develop a system that you consistently follow for taking and organizing your notes. One system recommends dividing your paper into two columns (a narrow one to the left of the paper and a wider one to the right). In the wide column labeled *Information,* place the notes you take during a class lecture or reading. In the left-hand column labeled *Recall,* write key words and phrases afterwards that will help you to recall the content.

■ Date your notes, record the course name, and number each page.

■ Try to summarize main ideas of the lecture in your own words.

■ Use any crutches you can to help (boxes around key ideas, drawings in the margin, colored inks, highlighters, your own shorthand).

■ Get permission to use a tape recorder with a counter on it; tape the whole lecture, but take notes as well. When you cannot keep up, put the number from the counter in your notes and leave a space. Later you can replay the missing parts of the lecture. This will save time.

■ Use a laptop computer to take notes.

Organization

If you want to be a successful student, you must take the time to plan and organize. Here are the critical habits you need to cultivate:

➲ Establish personal goals and priorities. What do you want to accomplish and what are you going to do first?

➲ Budget time effectively and meet deadlines.

➲ Develop a system for keeping track of assignment due dates.

➲ Have all of the materials you need to complete assignments.

➲ Develop a daily/weekly study schedule.

Problems with Reading

If you have any of these common reading problems, hire a reading tutor or sign up for a literacy class at your local public library. Anyone can get help and learn to read. It is never too late. Which of these characterize you?

◆ Difficulty with phonics

◆ Difficulty blending sounds

◆ Difficulty with sight-word recognition

◆ Difficulty reading accurately

◆ Reversing letters, numbers, or words

◆ Omitting letters or syllables

◆ Skipping over words or entire lines

◆ Difficulty understanding and/or remembering literal information

◆ Difficulty understanding and/or remembering inferential information

◆ Difficulty understanding and/or remembering applicative information

◆ Reading too slowly

Quantity and Quality Control

Those of us with attention and learning disorders have both quantity and quality control problems. If, as I do, you rush through your assignments to get them done, scarcely paying attention to the details or double-checking, you have a quality problem. But quantity problems are just as serious. These problems occur when you have a fixation on perfection, so you cannot ever get the whole thing done. Aim for a balance. Whether you finish the test first and get half the answers wrong or complete half the test and get all your answers right, your score will be the same—50 percent.

Reading Comprehension

Understanding what you read is crucial to academic success. Of course you need to be able to pronounce the words and know their meanings. But only when you can summarize the main idea of what the author is trying to communicate as well as understand and use the information are you truly comprehending what you read. You can improve your reading skills by practicing (see the hints that follow) and by using specific strategies (see the next section).

■ Read a lot. Practice will improve your reading skills. Read easy material for fun.

■ Build your vocabulary. Learn a new word every day. Write it on a three-by-five card along with its meaning and look at it several times each day.

■ Write down words you have trouble reading and say them to yourself each day.

■ If you have trouble understanding a story, read it again. Try reading it out loud to yourself.

■ Be aware of the specific purpose for which you are reading a selection (to find factual answers, to determine the main idea, to compare it to something else, or perhaps to critically evaluate it).

S trategies: Develop Your Own

Dr. Florence Haseltime, director of the Center for Population Research of the National Institute of Child Health and Human Development, states, "My motto is find out what you cannot do and discard it. Find another way."[4]

In *Seven Kinds of Smart,* Thomas Armstrong describes a game plan for "working with your weakest link." I have followed this format throughout my life, always looking for ways to compensate for my weaknesses. Armstrong suggests considering these questions as you develop strategies to help yourself. Be creative.

◆ How can I by-pass the problem using a technological aid?

◆ How can I by-pass the problem using an alternative symbol system, such as pictures rather than words?

◆ What sort of specialist could help me deal with this problem?

◆ What specific books, software programs, games, or other learning tools can I borrow, rent, or buy to help me deal with this issue?

◆ What personal qualities (such as courage, determination, persistence) do I need to develop to help me with this situation?

◆ What activities can I do to link areas of weakness with my areas of greatest strength?

◆ How can I get people around me to accommodate my learning needs so that this is no longer as much of a problem?

◆ What other things can I do to help cope with this difficulty?[5]

Tests, Tests, Tests

Here are my sure-fire test-taking strategies:

➲ Find a tutor to teach you how to take tests, and then take practice tests on your own.

> *When it comes to reading material, the point is not how fast you can get through the material, but how much of the material can get through to you.*
>
> —*Mortimer Adler*

➲ Obtain copies of previous tests and use them to prepare for your test. Try to figure out what the questions will be.

➲ Learn from your previous mistakes. After you have taken a test, go over it carefully and try to figure out why you made the mistakes you did. Was it a careless mistake? Did you make it because you did not study something you should have? Once you have figured out why you made the mistakes, you can do things differently before the next test.

➲ Ask for as much time as possible when taking a test.

➲ Study efficiently. Identify the important information and forget about the rest.

⊃ Study for shorter periods over a longer period of time. Do not cram.

⊃ If you are taking a multiple-choice or standardized test, work quickly. Such tests are timed, and students who move quickly, even if they pick some wrong answers, get better scores than students who know the material better but are slow at taking tests.

⊃ If you are taking a true-false test, read carefully. Every word is there for a reason. Watch for clue words. Researchers have found that if the words *all, only, always,* and *because* are in the question, chances are it is false. If the words *none, generally,* or *usually* are found, the question is generally true. Do not try to pick a fight or argue with the question. Maybe the true statement is only approximately true, but that is good enough for a true answer. Guess. If you do not know, you have a good chance of guessing right.

Effective Study Skills: A Step-by-Step System for Achieving Student Success by James K. Semones. Fort Worth, TX: Harcourt Brace Jovanovich, 1991.

Underachievement

"I was tested for the first time in seventh grade. My teacher told me I was really smart and could learn to read if I wanted to."
—*Teresa Lorenzen, 34, college student and mother, LD*

"I wasn't aware of my disability until the age of forty when a counselor at a rehabilitation hospital started asking me questions and suggested I be tested."
—*Marlene Jensen, 52, housewife, LD*

"I wasn't diagnosed until my midthirties. I have both ADHD and an auditory-processing problem that is very frustrating. Finally, I knew I wasn't stupid."
—*Kristina Howard, 42, housewife, ADHD and LD*

Underachievement is having the ability (intelligence) to achieve, but having a disability that temporarily short-circuits achievement. Those who have learning disorders can actually document their underachievement through testing. Individuals with learning disorders will score at an average or above-average intelligence level on a performance-based intelligence test that is nonverbal, while scoring way below average on tests that require reading, writing, or mathematics. As long as a learning disorder is undiagnosed, stupidity, lack of motivation, and laziness are cited as possible causes for failure to achieve.

Those of us with attention disorders have fewer avenues of documentation available to us via testing. Indeed, because we often can muster the attention and concentration to do well on an occasional test, or even through advanced study in school, we further confound the experts who are sure that if we really tried we could do this in all settings. Nevertheless, we are underachieving since our disorder is hampering the full use of our abilities.

Visual Learning

Compare yourself to the following list of descriptors to see if you are a visual learner. If so, then use the tips below to help you become a more effective learner. Play to your strengths rather than bemoaning your weaknesses.

■ You have a strong color sense.

■ You follow written directions well.

■ You have difficulty following lectures.

■ You process auditory input slowly.

■ You translate verbal input into pictures.

■ You need to closely watch a speaker's facial expression and body language.

■ You are particularly distracted by noise or people talking in the background.

■ You use visualization to help remember things.

■ You take notes with visual representations.

■ You know something by seeing it.

Tips for Visual Learners

1. Sign up for small classes where you can personally interact with the teacher.

2. Learn all you can about graphic organizers and use them whenever you take notes or study for tests.

3. Find a quiet place to study where noise and visual distractions are at a minimum.

4. Color-code your notes and files.

5. Hire a classmate to take notes from the class lectures for you.

Word Processing

This marvelous technology will enable you to hand in papers that are well written, well organized, and free from most spelling and grammar errors.

Cut, copy, paste, delete. There are dozens of computer-assisted-composing software programs. Some help you with outlining and structuring your writing assignments. Most programs are updated almost yearly, so visit the computer store, your local school, or the community college to check out what they are using in their computer labs.

X-ercise Your Rights

> "A disability should not be viewed as a way of getting out of something. We need to work harder to achieve."
> —*Teresa Lorenzen, 34, college student and mother, LD*

As mentioned in the last chapter, accommodations are modifications that are made to a work or school environment in order to make it "user-friendly" to people with disabilities. In education, accommodations can take many forms. Contrary to what many observers believe, accommodations do not require that course content or standards be lowered. Rather, accommodations are changes made and tested for their effectiveness in allowing students to learn. As you seek further education, find a school and teachers who are eager to make the modifications which the law requires. Do not settle for anything less.

Here are some accommodations to which you may be entitled as a student with an attention or learning disorder:

◆ access to computers inside as well as outside the classoom (to take notes, do homework, or take tests)

◆ access to tape recorders for taking notes

◆ access to calculators to speed up calculations

◆ access to tape recorded books to help with reading material

◆ extra time to take tests and do lab assignments

◆ oral rather than written tests

◆ tutoring in areas of need

◆ waiving of foreign-language requirements

◆ a reduced course load

◆ permission to take exams in a separate room with fewer distractions

◆ access to a single dormitory room to limit distractions if you are an on-campus student

Y esterday

Yesterday is the day by which everything should have been done. Do not put off until tomorrow what must be done today. Just remember:

⊃ We live in a credential-oriented society.

⊃ Those with the best education get the best jobs.

⊃ Career advancement today requires lifelong learning.

⊃ Decisions you make today will shape your future.

⊃ Grades are important.[6]

Z ero Hour

Zero hour is the crucial, decisive, or charged moment. It is the deadline, the moment of truth. Zero hour is the moment when you face your failures up to now as a student and make up your mind to:

◆ make your move

◆ take the ball on the rebound

◆ take a chance

◆ take advantage of the opportunity

My friend Sally and I were having a conversation about her future. She was trying to decide whether to pursue an advanced degree at the age of forty-five. "I'll be fifty before I finish," she lamented.

"How old will you be in five years if you don't do it?" I asked.

"Fifty," she answered sheepishly.

Do not just talk about it. Get help. Learn to read. Enroll in a class. Avail yourself of the accommodations you have coming to you. Take the plunge.

7

The ABCs of Living Fully

The Spiritual Connection

A recurring theme in my conversations with the many individuals I interviewed in the preparation of this book has been the power they have found in faith and spiritual renewal. They spoke of the help it gave them not only in dealing with the daily frustrations of attention and learning disorders but also in healing the pain remaining from past hurts.

This chapter highlights the part that our spiritual life can play in overcoming and coping with attention and learning disorders. It is the most personal chapter of this book because I include details of my own faith journey. For a significant portion of my adult life, I denied my spiritual needs and turned my back on organized religion. However, the recognition in my early forties that my life was out of control brought me to my knees both literally and figuratively. I came to the realization that I could not do it all on my own. Then, as I turned to God for forgiveness and healing, I also learned that many of the practices of my faith (meditation, prayer, solitude, study, confession) were also very helpful in dealing with aspects of my attention disorder.

Whether you embrace the Christian faith (as I do) or another faith tradition or have no traditional faith, I hope the following sections will prove helpful to you.

A nger and Abandonment

> Sometimes I feel like a motherless child,
> Sometimes I feel like a motherless child,
> Sometimes I feel like a motherless child,
> A long way from home.
>
> Sometimes I feel like I'm almost gone,
> Sometimes I feel like I'm almost gone,
> Sometimes I feel like I'm almost gone,
> Way up to that heavenly land,
> Way up to that heavenly land.
> —*African American spiritual*

When our life is in total chaos, it is tempting to fall into the trap of feeling abandoned by friends, family, and even our faith. How does one avoid this trap?

Remember that no one is exempt from problems and difficulties. As Rabbi Harold S. Kushner points out in his book *When Bad Things Happen to Good People,* there are no exceptions for nice people. Faith does not shelter you from difficulty; its gift is the enabling power it grants you to handle adversity with peace, grace, hope, and calm.

Do not use the difficult times that come into your life as an excuse or reason for abandoning your faith. The most magnificent example of this principle is the Old Testament character Job. The troubles in Job's life make you want to weep. Yet this amazing man did not abandon his faith. He is an ancient example for us of how to cope in the face of overwhelming tragedy and adversity.

B usyness

Mary and Martha are notable biblical sisters whose contrasting personalities and lifestyles have often provided lessons for my life. They were friends of Jesus Christ and frequently entertained him together in their home. But their approaches to socializing with the most famous teacher of the day differed greatly. On one occasion, Jesus gently chides Martha for her anxious and worried demeanor as she bustles about from job to job. Her sister, Mary, he points out, has chosen to sit with Jesus, giving him her undivided attention and interest. Whether or not Martha may have had an attention disorder as evidenced by her problems with sitting still and concentrating on a conversation, the lesson for me has been the importance of taking time to focus on my spouse, my children, and my friends . . . to sit with them and listen, to spend time with them, and to leave my ever growing list of "things to do" on the shelf for an hour or two.

C onfession

Revealing our failures and shortcomings to another is very difficult. I approach this process feeling either totally superior (Why should I admit my problems to someone who is no angel?) or completely abject (This person is a saint—I cannot air my dirty laundry in this esteemed company). I make a habit of personally making my confession to God, but the process must often take place with my friends and family as well. I have a terrible time with confession. I want to be perfect, and when I do not confess, I can fool myself into believing this lie. The beautiful thing about confession is the freedom and joy it brings to my heart and mind.

D iscipline

In *Celebration of Discipline,* Richard Foster writes about the spiritual "exercises" that can help us focus on God:

> God intends the Disciplines of the spiritual life to be for ordinary human beings: people who have jobs, who care for children, who wash dishes and mow lawns. In fact, the Disciplines are best exercised in the midst of our relationships with our husband or wife, our brothers and sisters, our friends and neighbors.[1]

The disciplines of the spiritual life are doubly difficult for those of us with attention and learning disorders. Meditation, study, solitude, and submission do not come easily at all. But the wonder of truly embracing these disciplines is that we need not rely on personal will power, determination, and self-discipline. We need only to place ourselves before God so that he can transform us.

Celebration of Discipline: The Path to Spiritual Growth by Richard Foster. San Francisco: HarperSan Francisco, 1988.

Encouragement and Affirmation

Affirmation is a powerful tool for bringing about change in your attitudes and behavior. People with attention and learning disorders have lived with so much criticism, they tend to discount affirmation. Be open and receptive to words of encouragement and love. Here are some suggestions for making encouragement more a part of your life:

> *The confession of evil works is the first beginning of good works.*
>
> —*Augustine*

◆ Spend time with people who affirm you. Seek them out and cultivate relationships with them. Spend as little time as possible with individuals who criticize, tear down, and undermine you.

◆ Rejoice in your uniqueness as a human being. Jeanie Miley suggests affirmations such as the following: God is creating a new heart within me; I am loved and forgiven by God; *Emmanuel* means "God is with me."

◆ Do not confuse affirmations (whether given by others, God, or yourself) and your personal feelings about the affirmation. When you feel hypocritical or dishonest in making the affirmations, Miley suggests asking God to close the space between what is true and what you desire to be true (or between what is true and what you fail to recognize as truth).

The Spiritual Art of Creative Silence: Lessons in Christian Meditation by Jeanie Miley. Wheaton, IL: Harold Shaw Publishers, 1996.

F orgiveness

Charles Stanley says that

> Forgiveness is never completed until, first, we have experienced the forgiveness of God, second, we can forgive others who have wronged us, and third, we are able to forgive ourselves.[2]

Forgiveness is the healing balm that soothes the angry wounds and open sores that irritate and debilitate our lives. Forgiveness needs to be spread wherever there is pain, and the process must happen at many levels for its restorative properties to be fully realized.

⊃ Accept forgiveness from God. He knows us intimately and loves us. He accepts us as we are and extends forgiveness for all that we have done and will do.

⊃ Forgive yourself. This can be a difficult process. But dredging up stupid mistakes, failed relationships, and misguided motivations is not productive. Stop beating up on yourself and move on.

⊃ Forgive others—family, friends, and teachers—for the ways they have treated you.

⊃ Ask for forgiveness from those whom you have hurt with your impulsive actions, addictive lifestyle, or hasty words.

G oodness and Mercy

At the times of my life when I have been the most desolate and despairing, the words of Psalm 23 have been truly healing. In one of my darkest hours, I repeated this psalm over and over, scarcely aware of what was happening to my body. Lying prone, I became aware of strong arms coming underneath to hold and cradle me. This sensation was remarkably real, and although at no time since have I felt this again, I know those arms are still there.

> *Surely goodness and mercy shall follow me all the days of my life.*
>
> —*Psalm 23:6*

H ealing Activities

When you are hurting, there is need for healing. This healing can happen by means of a variety of activities; choose those that best meet your needs:[3]

journaling
support groups
reading
listening to speakers
praying or meditating
training in time-management
   or problem-solving skills
workshops on forgiveness
spiritual retreats
art therapy
sex therapy

individual counseling
deep individual therapy
intensive group therapy
intensive couples therapy
intensive family therapy
in- or outpatient treatment
   programs focused on
   detoxification
interpersonal-relationship
   training
career assessment

I magination

A theologian writes about the imagination,

> There was a time when visionaries were canonized, and mystics were admired. Now they are studied, smiled at, perhaps even committed. All in all, fantasy is viewed with distrust in our times.[4]

Use your imagination to celebrate your uniqueness. Write poetry;

sing songs; paint pictures. Do not be embarrassed to express your spiritual side through the arts. My friend Carolyn Dietering is a liturgical dancer who brings faith alive through movement. She also wrote the beautiful poem included in the Memories section in this chapter.

J ournals

Writing in *How to Keep a Spiritual Journal,* Ronald Klug states,

> A journal is a tool for self-discovery, an aid to concentration, a mirror for the soul, a place to generate and capture ideas, a safety valve for the emotions, a training ground for the writer, and a good friend and confidant.[5]

Here are just a few of the benefits that journal writing can bring to those who write regularly. Writing in a journal helps you . . .

- clarify your personal goals, keep them before you, and move steadily toward achieving them

- make the best possible use of your time

- establish a clear sense of priorities

- manage your time to achieve God's purpose for your life

- understand your past

- make decisions

- cope with anger and depression

- improve your writing and thinking skills in a nonthreatening, unpressured way. This is especially important for those with learning disorders who need regular practice.

How to Keep a Spiritual Journal: A Guide to Journal Keeping for Inner Growth and Personal Discovery by Ronald Klug. Minneapolis: Augsburg, 1993.

Koinonia

This Greek word suggests a deep, inward "meeting of the minds and spirits" that occurs when people gather together to worship as one body. Experiencing this sense of unity within a like-minded group can achieve what Thomas Kelly describes when he writes:

> A quickening Presence pervades us, breaking down some part of the special privacy and isolation of our individual lives and blending our spirits within a superindividual Life and Power. An objective dynamic Presence enfolds us all, nourishes our souls, speaks glad, unutterable comfort with us, and quickens us in depths that had before been slumbering.[6]

This sense of unity is what keeps me returning to worship each week to receive the sacraments and the Word. This "meeting of the minds" helps me to forgive the foibles of my fellow worshipers and to make organized religion a regular part of my spiritual growth.

Limitations

I am encouraged by the fact that God included people in biblical history who had limitations and were not perfect. That means there is a place for me. "Noah got drunk, Moses got angry, and Gideon got scared. Peter could be inconsistent, Paul was inconsiderate, Thomas doubted, Martha pouted," Stuart Briscoe says.[7] I wonder if any of these biblical folk had attention or learning disorders. Sure sounds like the symptoms to me.

Memories

Carolyn Dietering writes,

> I never told anyone
> that I was the one
> who spilled the cocoa

in Margie's blue rabbit slipper.
She had gone upstairs awhile
and I was left alone
in her basement playroom
with my steaming mug.
Daddy always swirled his cocoa—
some movement of the wrist
replacing the need of a spoon.
I thought that quite grown up.
My wrist began to turn.
The cocoa began to move
higher and higher toward the rim—
I tried to stem the tide.
But soon, too late, it was all over
my hand, my pinafore, my shoe,
I was again a little girl,
not at all like Daddy.
Worst of all, near where I stood,
the rabbit slipper steamed—
cocoa drenched, its ears collapsed.
I gripped the mug in vain.
As Margie came back down the stairs,
my mind was white with fear.
"I have to go now. I can't play any more."
I turned to take my leave.
Behind my back, the rabbit still breathed
its blueness chocolate brown.
I never did learn Daddy's trick.
Today I use a spoon.[8]

The experiences of childhood stay with us in vivid memories like this one:

> "I remember the day almost as if it was yesterday. It was on a Tuesday, and I was in kindergarten. As I watched in horror, Jamie proceeded to wipe his "booger" on me! I nudged him and told him to quit. He then decided that I needed a good pinch. I screamed in pain. What came next, I will never forget, because

from that moment on, I knew I was naughty and disruptive. Miss K. gave me and Jamie hard smacks on our little bottoms, in front of the entire class. I was never so ashamed and embarrassed in my entire life. And from then on, I knew I was bad."

—*Jessica Beacon, 16, high school student, ADHD*

Unlocking childhood memories can often be a powerful tool for better understanding ourselves and putting behind us experiences that still make us feel unhappy, used, incompetent, and bad. Use your journal, find a good therapist, or share memories with a friend.

ow

A perusal of *Roget's Thesaurus* for synonyms for the words *past, present,* and *future* reveals something to me about the way we humans approach the living of our lives. There are almost two columns of words that can be used in writing and conversation to refer to the past. Nearly the same number of synonyms can be found for the word *future.* But for the word *present,* the time on which we should be focusing and attending, there is slightly less than a column of synonyms. We often do not focus on the now. Instead, we spend too much time dwelling on the past and worrying about the future.

> *Carpe diem.*
> *(Seize the day.)*

O penness

I was once a very close-minded and opinionated person. I felt free to criticize and judge but felt no obligation to receive opinions and feedback from others. I can give no other explanation for my change of heart than my faith.

I urge you to remain open to how God may be leading you to change and grow. Respond to the people he sends into your life to help you mature. Ask for God's help in battering down the defensiveness and close-mindedness that may keep you from hearing what God (and your friends and family) may be trying to say to you. ◦

 rayer

This prayer appears on an altar at the Vatican:

> Our Father, grant us, this day, the sense of your presence to cheer us, and your light to direct us, and give us strength for your service. We are only little children, and the world seems very dark to us, and our path very hard, if we are alone. But we know we can come to our Father, to ask you to help us, and enliven us, and strengthen us, and give us hope.

Prayer is a powerful tool for gaining access to the power of God to heal our bodies, minds, and souls. Richard Foster says that "to pray is to change."[9] For those of us with attention and learning disorders who want desperately to change, this statement holds the promise of help for our disordered, distracted, and unfulfilled lives. Here are some suggestions from Susan and Jay Trygstad[10] on how to focus your prayers if praying is an unfamiliar experience for you:

⊃ Focus your prayer on a single word that represents God for you (such as Jesus, Father, Spirit, Lord). Say this word over and over silently in your mind. Use this word to bring yourself into an awareness of the presence of God.

⊃ Pray by reading short passages of Scripture, speaking the Word back to God while listening intently for God to speak to you.

⊃ Pray while taking your daily walk.

⊃ Pray the prayer of relinquishment in which you turn your most desperate situation over to God and entrust yourself to his wisdom, power, and love.

And here are some thoughts on prayer from Richard Foster that may surprise you:

- The Bible speaks of God changing his mind. We can work with God to determine the future. That should motivate you to pray!

- Try flash praying—saying a prayer for a stranger in an airline terminal or a homeless person to whom you make a donation.

- Never wait until you feel like praying—it is work that must be done like any other work.

Praying for Wholeness and Healing by Richard J. Beckman. Minneapolis: Augsburg, 1994.

Quiet Times

Richard Foster writes in *Celebration of Discipline,*

> If we are constantly being swept off our feet with frantic activity, we will be unable to be attentive at the moment of inward silence.[11]

Above all, we need quiet times in our lives. Although we crave excitement, interruptions, and movement, it is in times of quiet that we can hear what is being said (by others and by God), sense what is being felt (by ourselves and by those we love), and experience the present (rather than dwelling on the past or racing ahead to the future). Turn off the radio. Pull the plug on your TV. Shut your mouth. Stop racing about and be quiet.

Reconciliation

This word speaks to me of mending fences, of negotiating truces, of healing hurts. I have done some reconciling in the past few years, and it feels good. It feels so much better than the separation, the distance, and the sense of superiority that characterized my former stance. I can say with certainty that if you have attention and learning disorders, there are folks with whom you need to reconcile. You can choose to do it now; you can choose to do it later; or you can have the choice made for you when the person with whom you need to reconcile dies.

S olitude and Meditation

In *Spiritual Direction and Meditation,* Thomas Merton wrote,

> Meditation is not so much a way to find God as it is a way of resting in Him whom we have found, who loves us, who is near to us, who comes to draw us to Himself.[12]

Meditation is a time-honored practice of spiritual giants. Christian meditation is, according to Richard Foster, "the ability to hear God's voice and obey his word."[13] In addition to its spiritual benefits, meditation has helped many people overcome addictions, sleep disorders, depression, and anxiety. Further, meditation has been shown to improve creativity, concentration, mental alertness, and memory.

Unfortunately, meditating is not a practice that comes easily to those of us with attention and learning disorders. Meditation is best carried on in a quiet and contemplative environment. We crave action and interruptions. Meditation involves focus on a single idea or phrase. Our minds dart off in a thousand directions. Meditation requires a relaxation of body. We are tapping our fingers and toes, all the while restlessly moving about in our chairs. Meditation will require discipline but will pay rich dividends. Here are some suggestions:

- Establish a routine and find a place that will be consistently private and quiet.

- Sit in a comfortable position with both feet flat on the floor in a straight-backed chair.

- Close your eyes to remove distractions and center on the object of your meditation.

- Consciously relax your body's muscles.

- Clear your mind of worries and frustrations.

- Focus for ten to twenty minutes on a single prayer or verse. Repeat it silently or see it in your mind's eye each time you exhale.

- Assume a passive attitude regarding distracting thoughts. Without distress, disregard them and return to the prayer or verse you have selected. Be relaxed in dealing with these interrupting thoughts, but always return to the focus of your meditation.

- Psalm 23, Psalm 100, and Psalm 46 are excellent Scripture portions for meditation.

- Picture God taking delight in you.

- Be patient in your practice of meditation. Richard Foster says that "it is not a single act nor can it be completed the way one completes building a chair. It is a way of life."[14]

Celebration of Discipline by Richard Foster. San Francisco: HarperSan Francisco, 1988.

Time

One of the bits of wisdom contained in *Life's Little Instruction Book* is this:

> Don't say you don't have enough time. You have exactly the same number of hours per day that were given to Helen Keller, Pasteur, Michelangelo, Mother Teresa, Leonardo da Vinci, Thomas Jefferson, and Albert Einstein.[15]

How do you find the time to include in your life all of these wonderful things for your soul, such as meditation, solitude, quietness, and study? There are not any easy answers, I know that. I fight the constant battle between calm and chaos myself. But do not give up. Schedule it, plan for it, and take it.

U ncluttered

This is my goal—to have a life that is simple, basic, essential, and fundamental; to be real, to be uncomplicated, to be uncorrupted and undiluted. Attention deficit disorder constantly mitigates against my goal. I say yes when I should say no. I prevaricate when I should be straightforward. I make it complicated when it should be simple. But I will not give up. I still want to be uncluttered and pure.

V ision

Do you have a vision for what you would like your life to be? Do you have goals to accompany that vision? Goals for your career? Goals for your family life? Goals for your spiritual growth? Goals for your social and educational development? There is an Old Testament warning that says "without a vision, the people perish." We can personalize that phrase and say "without a vision, the individual will hit a dead end." What is your vision? Write it down. Talk about it with a trusted friend. Take the first step in reaching one of your goals.

W ake-Up Calls

David and Rebecca Grudermeyer and Lerissa Nancy Patrick[16] describe wake-up calls as happenings in our lives that force us to pay attention to a particularly destructive course of action we are following. I believe these wake-up calls come from God. Depending on how carefully we are listening, we may hear even his faintest whisper. But there are those of us (myself included) who need a cataclysmic alarm. Does this description hit home with you? "A resistant denial-ridden learner needs more intense wake-up calls, such as accidents, arrests, illness, life-threatening disease, getting fired, losing relationships, hitting bottom with addictions."[17] Now is the time to pay attention to the wake-up calls you may be receiving. Whether they be small mishaps or major, life-threatening events, listen up. Get help today.

X-amine **Y** ourself

Self-examination and reflection do not come easily to those of us with attention and learning disorders. We are easily distracted, often bored, and not very thoughtful. Personal growth, however, is not possible without self-examination. Here are some steps to get you started:

> *The life which is unexamined is not worth living.*
>
> —*Socrates*

➲ Think about what you are going to do before you do it. Does a small voice inside your head caution you about the common sense, good judgment, or wisdom of doing it? If so, stop.

➲ Think about what you are doing while you are doing it. If you engage in what psychologists call metacognition (stepping back mentally while you are engaged physically), you may have time to redirect, refocus, or change your direction entirely.

➲ Think about what you have done after you have done it. Do you want to repeat this behavior again? Was it worthwhile? Did it help you? Did it benefit somebody else? Was it a waste of time?

➲ Think about how you might do it differently the next time, if necessary.

Z ing

I hope that as you have read this book you have found the lively, zestful quality I promised you in chapter 1. Please write me if you have found this book to be helpful or if you have new strategies to share in a forthcoming book.

> Elaine K. McEwan
> c/o Harold Shaw Publishers
> P.O. Box 567
> Wheaton, IL 60189

Appendix

Resources for Individuals and Their Families

Organizations That Offer Information, Support, and Advocacy

Attention Deficit Disorder Association (ADDA)
P.O. Box 972
Mentor, OH 44061
800-487-2282

Attention Deficit Information Network (AD-IN)
475 Hillside Avenue
Needham, MA 02194
617-455-9895

CH.A.D.D. (Children and Adults with Attention Deficit Disorders)
National Headquarters
499 NW 70th Avenue
Suite 308
Plantation, FL 33317
954-587-3700
(CH.A.D.D. has local chapters throughout the United States. Locations, contact names, and phone numbers are available through National Headquarters.)

Council for Exceptional Children
1920 Association Drive
Reston, VA 22091-1589
703-264-9474
800-328-0272
Fax 703-264-9494

Health Resource Center
(National Clearinghouse for Postsecondary Education for People with
    Disabilities)
1 DuPont Circle NW
Washington, D.C. 20036

Learning Disabilities Association
4156 Library Road
Pittsburgh, PA 15234
412-341-1515

National Center for Learning Disabilities
99 Park Avenue
New York, NY 10016
212-545-7510

NICCHY (National Information Center for Children and Youth with
    Disabilities)
P.O. Box 1492
Washington, D.C. 20013
800-695-0285

National Network of Learning Disabled Adults (NNLDA)
808 North 82nd Street, Suite F2
Scottsdale, AZ 85257
602-941-5112

Orton Dyslexia Society (ODS)
8600 La Salle Road
Chester Building, Suite 382
Towson, MD 21204
800-222-3123
301-296-0232

Project Literacy U.S. (PLUS)
4802 Fifth Avenue
Pittburgh, PA 15213
412-622-1491

U.S. Department of Education Office of Vocational and Adult Education:
    Division of Clearinghouse on Adult Education
MES Building, Room 4416
400 Maryland Avenue SW
Washington, D.C. 20202-5515
202-732-2410

Periodicals, Pamphlets, and Newsletters

Career Development for Exceptional Individuals
1920 Association Drive
Reston, VA 22091

Challenge (ADHD Newsletter)
P.O. Box 488
West Newbury, MA 01985
508-462-0495

College HELPS Newsletter
Partners in Publishing
Box 50347
Tulsa, OK 74150
918-584-5906

Journal of Learning Disabilities
PRO-ED
8700 Shoal Creek Rd.
Austin, TX 78758-6897
512-451-3246

LDA Newsbriefs
4156 Library Road
Pittsurgh, PA 15234
412-341-1515

Learning Disabilities: A Multidisciplinary Journal
4156 Library Road
Pittsburgh, PA 15234
412-341-1515

Learning Disabilities Research and Practice
1920 Reston Drive
Reston, VA 22091
703-620-3660

Learning Disability Quarterly
Council for Learning Disabilities
Box 40303
Overland Park, KS 66204
913-492-8755

National Network of LD Adults Newsletter (NNLDA)
808 North 82nd Street, Suite F2
Scottsdale, AZ 85257
602-941-5112

Perspectives on Dyslexia
8600 La Salle Road
Chester Building, Suite 382
Towson, MD 21204
301-296-0232

Advocacy Organizations

Bazelon Center for Mental Health Law
1101 15th Street NW
Suite 1212
Washington, D.C. 20005-5002
202-467-5730   TTY 202-467-4232

Center for Law and Education, Inc.
955 Massachusetts Avenue
Cambridge, MA 02139

DREDF (Disabilities Rights Education and Defense Fund, Inc.)
1616 P Street NW
Suite 100
Washington, D.C. 20036

National Council on Disability
800 Independence Avenue SW
Suite 814
Washington, D.C. 20591
202-267-3846   TTY 202-267-3232

NPND (National Parent Network on Disability)
1600 Prince Street
Suite 115
Alexandria, VA 22314
703-684-6763
(NPND has a listing of parent networks throughout the United States. They will
mail or fax it to you upon request.)

United States Government Agencies

For questions about IDEA and PL 94-142 call or write to:
U.S. Department of Education
Office of Special Education Programs
400 Maryland Avenue SW
Washington, D.C. 20202
202-205-5507

For questions about Section 504 call or write to:
U.S. Department of Education
Office for Civil Rights
400 Maryland Avenue SW
Washington, D.C. 20202
202-732-1635

For questions about Americans with Disabilities Act (ADA) call or write to:

Regarding discrimination:
EEOC (Equal Employment Opportunity Commission)
1801 L Street NW
Washington, D.C. 20507
800-669-4000

Regarding accommodations:
United States Department of Justice
Civil Rights Division
P.O. Box 66118
Washington, D.C. 20035-6118
800-669-3362

Department of Education Office for Civil Rights: Regional Civil Rights Offices

Region I: Connecticut, Maine, Massachusetts, New Hampshire, Rhode Island, Vermont

Regional Civil Rights Director
Office for Civil Rights, Region I
U.S. Department of Education
John W. McCormick Post Office and Court House—Room 222
Post Office Square
Boston, MA 02109
617-223-1154   TTY 617-223-1111

Region II: New Jersey, New York, Puerto Rico, Virgin Islands

Regional Civil Rights Director
Office for Civil Rights, Region II
U.S. Department of Education
26 Federal Plaza, R33-130
New York, NY 10278
212-264-5180 TTY 212-264-9464

Region III: Delaware, District of Columbia, Maryland, Pennsylvania, Virginia, West Virginia

Regional Civil Rights Director
Office for Civil Rights, Region III
U.S. Department of Education
Gateway Building, 3535 Market Street
P.O. Box 13716
Philadelphia, PA 19101
215-596-6772   TTY 215-596-6794

Region IV: Alabama, Florida, Georgia, Kentucky, Mississippi, North Carolina, South Carolina, Tennesssee

Regional Civil Rights Director
Office for Civil Rights, Region IV
U.S. Department of Education
101 Marietta Tower, Room 2702
Atlanta, GA 30323
404-221-2954   TTY 404-221-2010

Region V: Illinois, Indiana, Minnesota, Michigan, Ohio, Wisconsin

Regional Civil Rights Director
Office for Civil Rights, Region V
U.S. Department of Education
300 South Wacker Drive, 8th Floor
Chicago, IL 60606
312-353-2520   TTY 312-353-2520

Region VI: Arkansas, Louisiana, New Mexico, Oklahoma, Texas

Regional Civil Rights Director
Office for Civil Rights, Region VI
U.S. Department of Education
1200 Main Tower Building, Room 1935
Dallas, TX 75202
214-676-3951 TTY 214-767-6599

Region VII: Iowa, Kansas, Missouri, Nebrasks

Regional Civil Rights Director
Office for Civil Rights, Region VII
U.S. Department of Education
324 E. 11th Street, 24th Floor
Kansas City, MO 64106
816-374-2223 TTY 816-374-7264

Region VIII: Colorado, Montana, North Dakota, South Dakota, Utah, Wyoming

Regional Civil Rights Director
Office for Civil Rights, Region VIII
U.S. Department of Education
Federal Office Building
1961 Stout Street, Room 1185
Denver, CO 80294
303-884-5695 TTY 303-844-3417

Region IX: Arizona, California, Hawaii, Nevada, Guam, Trust Territory of the
Pacific Islands, American Samoa

Regional Civil Rights Director
Office for Civil Rights, Region IX
U.S. Department of Education
1275 Market Street, 14th Floor
San Francisco, CA 94103
415-556-9894 TTY 415-556-1933

Region X: Alaska, Idaho, Oregon, Washington

Regional Civil Rights Director
Office for Civil Rights, Region X
U.S. Department of Education
2901 3rd Avenue, Mail Stop 106
Seattle, WA 98121
206-442-1636 TTY 206-442-4542

Bibliography

You may find the following resources interesting. They have informed my writing, though I do not necessarily recommend each of them.

Armstrong, Thomas. *The Myth of the ADD Child: 50 Ways to Improve Your Child's Behavior and Attention Span Without Drugs, Labels, or Coercion.* New York: Penguin Books, 1995.

Armstrong, Thomas. *Seven Kinds of Smart.* New York: Penguin Books, 1993.

Aslett, Don. *How to Have a 48-Hour Day.* Cincinatti: Betterway Books, 1996.

Bain, Lisa J. *A Parent's Guide to Attention Deficit Disorders.* New York: Dell Publishing, 1991.

Barkley, Russell A. *Atention-Deficit Hyperactivity Disorder: A Handbook for Diagnosis and Treatment.* New York: Guilford Press, 1990.

Barnes, Emilie. *The Creative Home Organizer.* Eugene, OR: Harvest House Publishers, 1988.

Bassett, Lucinda. *From Panic to Power: Proven Techniques to Calm Your Anxieties, Conquer Your Fears, and Put You in Control of Your Life.* New York: HarperCollins, 1995.

Benson, Herbert. *Beyond the Relaxation Response.* New York: Times Books, 1984.

_____. *The Relaxation Response.* New York: William Morrow and Company, In., 1975.

Bliss, Edwin C. *Getting Things Done: The ABC's of Time Management.* New York: Scribner, 1991.

Bolles, Richard N. *What Color Is Your Parachute?* Berkeley, CA: Ten Speed Press, 1994.

Browne, Jackson H. *Life's Little Instruction Book.* Nashville, TN: Rutledge Hill Press, 1991.

Buzan, Tony. *Use Both Sides of Your Brain.* New York: Penguin Books, 1989.

Campbell, Jeff, and The Clean Team. *Speed Cleaning.* New York: Bantam Doubleday Dell Publishing Group, 1985.

Cherry, Clare; Douglas Godwin; and Jesse Staples. *Is the Left Brain Always Right?* New York: Fearon Teacher Aids, 1989.

Cook, Marshall J. *Slow Down and Get More Done.* Cincinnati, OH: Better Way Books, 1993.

Covey, Stephen; A. Roger Merrill; and Rebecca Merrill. *First Things First: To Live, To Love, To Learn, To Leave a Legacy.* New York: Simon & Shuster, 1994.

Culp, Stephanie. *How to Get Organized When You Don't Have the Time.* Cincinatti, OH: Writer's Digest Books, 1987.

Deitering, Carolyn. *I Am a Pilgrim Child.* Mystic, CT: Twenty-Third Publications, 1992.

Dominguez, Joe, and Vicki Robin. *Your Money or Your Life.* New York: Viking Penguin, 1992.

Eisenberg, Ronni, and Kate Kelly. *Organize Yourself.* New York: Macmillan, 1986.

Fadley, Jack L., and Virginia N. Hosler. *Attentional Deficit Disorder in Children and Adolescents.* Springfield, IL: Charles C. Thomas Publisher, 1992.

Foster, Richard. *Celebration of Discipline.* San Francisco: HarperSan Francisco, 1988.

Fowler, Rick, and Jerilyn Fowler. *"Honey, Are You Listening?" How Attention Deficit Could Be Affecting Your Marriage.* Nashville: Thomas Nelson, 1995.

Gale, Barry, and Linda Gale. *Stay or Leave.* New York: Harper & Row, 1989.

Garber, Stephen; Marianne Daniels Garber; and Robyn Freedman Spizmn. *Beyond Ritalin.* New York: Villard Books, 1996.

Gardner, Howard. *Multiple Intelligences: The Theory in Practice.* New York: Basic Books, 1993.

Gerber, Paul J., and Henry B. Reiff. *Speaking for Themselves: Ethnographic Interviews with Adults with Learning Disabilities.* Ann Arbor: Univ. of Michigan Press, 1991.

Giordano, Gerard. *Literacy: Programs for Adults with Developmental Disabilities.* San Diego: Singular Publishing Group, 1996.

Gregg, Noel; Cheri Hoy; and Alice F. Gay. *Adults with Learning Disabilities: Theoretical and Practical Perspectives.* New York: The Guilford Press, 1996.

Grudermeyer, David; Rebecca Grudermeyer; and Lerissa Nancy Patrick. *Sensible Self-Help: The First Road Map for the Healing Journey.* Del Mar, CA: Willingness Works Press, 1995.

Hall, David E. *Living with Learning Disabilities: A Guide for Students.* Minneapolis: Lerner Publications Company, 1993.

Hallowell, Edward, and John Ratey. *Anwers to Distraction.* New York: Pantheon, 1994.

_____. *Driven to Distraction.* New York: Pantheon, 1994.

Harrington, Thomas F. *Handbook of Career Planning for Special Needs Students.* Rockville, MD: Aspen Systems Corporation, 1982.

Hartmann, Thom. *ADD Success Stories: A Guide to Fulfillment for Families with Attention Deficit Disorder.* Grass Valley, CA: Underwood Books, 1995.

_____. *Attention Deficit Disorder: A Different Perception.* Grass Valley, CA: Underwood Books, 1993.

_____. *Focus Your Energy: Hunting for Success in Business with Attention Deficit Disorder.* New York: Pocket Books, 1994.

Hedrick, Lucy. *5 Days to an Organized Life.* New York: Dell Publishing, 1990.

Ingersoll, Barbara D., and Sam Goldstein. *Attention Deficit Disorder and Learning Disabilities: Realities, Myths and Controversial Treatments.* New York: Doubleday, 1993.

Johnston, Robert. *Attention Deficits, Learning Disabilities, and Ritalin: A Practical Guide.* San Diego: Singular Publishing Group, 1991.

Kabat-Zinn, Jon. *Wherever You Go There You Are: Mindfulness Meditation in Everyday Life.* New York: Hyperion, 1994.

Kelly, Kate, and Peggy Ramundo. *You Mean I'm Not Lazy, Stupid or Crazy?!* Cincinnati: Quality Books, 1994.

Keyes, Ralph. *Timelock: How Life Got So Hectic and What You Can Do About It.* New York: HarperCollins, 1991.

Kirsta, Alix. *The Book of Stress Survival.* New York: Simon & Schuster, 1986.

Klug, Ronald. *How to Keep a Spiritual Journal: A Guide to Journal Keeping for Inner Growth and Personal Discovery.* Minneapolis: Augsburg, 1993.

Koziol, Leonard F.; Chris E. Stout; and Douglas H. Ruben (eds.) *Handbook of Childhood Impulse Disorders and ADHD: Theory and Practice.* Springfield, IL: Charles C. Thomas Publisher, 1993.

Krauss, Pesach, and Morrie Goldfinger. *Why Me? Coping with Grief, Loss, and Change.* New York: Bantam Books, 1988.

Kushner, Harold S. *When Bad Things Happen to Good People.* New York: Avon Books, 1981.

Lakein, Alan. *How to Get Control of Your Time and Your Life.* New York: David McKay, 1973.

Lapp, Danielle C. *Don't Forget: Easy Exercises for a Better Memory at Any Age.* New York: McGraw Hill Book Company, 1987.

Lazear, David. *Seven Pathways of Learning: Teaching Students and Parents about Multiple Intelligences.* Tucson, AZ: Zephyr Press, 1994.

_____. *Seven Ways of Knowing.* Palatine, IL: IRI/Skylight Publihing, 1994.

Levinson, Harold N. *Smart, but Feeling Dumb.* New York: Warner Books, 1984.

_____. *Total Concentration: How to Understand Attention Deficit Disorder with Treatment Guidelines for You and Your Doctor.* New York: M. Evans and Company, 1990.

Lew, Irvina Siegel. *You Can't Do It All.* New York: Atheneum, 1986.

Lorayne, Harry, and Jerry Lucas. *The Memory Book.* New York: Ballatine Books, 1974.

McEwan, Elaine K. *Attention Deficit Disorder.* Wheaton, IL: Harold Shaw Publishers, 1996.

_____. *Solving School Problems.* Wheaton, IL: Harold Shaw Publishers, 1992.

McKenna, Alexis. *Doodling Your Way to Better Recall.* Tucson, AZ: Zephyr Press, 1979.

Mangrum, Charles T., II, and Stephen S. Strichart. *College and the Learning Disabled Student: A Guide to Program Selection, Development, and Implementation.* Orlando, FL: Grune & Stratton, 1984.

Miley, Jeanie. *The Spiritual Art of Creative Silence: Lessons in Christian Meditation.* Wheaton, IL: Harold Shaw Publishers, 1996.

Minirth, Frank, States Skipper, and Paul Meier. *100 Ways to Overcome Depression.* Grand Rapids, MI: Baker Books, 1995.

Montague, Marjorie. *Computers, Cognition, and Writing Instruction.* Albany: State Univ. of New York Press, 1990.

Morrison, Jaydene. *Coping with ADD/ADHD.* New York: The Rosen Publishing Group, 1996.

Murphy, Kevin R., and Suzanne LeVert. *Out of the Fog: Treatment Options and Coping Strategies for Adult Attention Deficit Disorder.* New York: Hyperion, 1995

Nadeau, Kathleen G. Ed. *A Comprehensive Guide to Attention Deficit Disorder in Adults: Research, Diagnosis, and Treatment.* New York: Brunner/Mazel Publishers, 1995.

Peck, M. Scott. *The Road Less Traveled.* New York: Simon & Schuster, 1978.

Peurifoy, Reneau. *Anxiety, Phobias, and Panic.* New York: Warner Books, 1995.

Phelan, Thomas, dir. *Adults with Attention Deficit Disorder.* Video. Child Management, Inc., Glen Ellyn, IL, 1994.

Pine, David J. *365 Good Health Hints.* Carson, CA: Hay House, 1994.

Quinn, Patricia O. Ed. *ADD and the College Student.* New York: Magination Press, 1994.

Quinn, Patricia O., and Judith M. Stern. *Putting on the Brakes: Young People's Guide to Understanding Attention Deficit Hyperactivity Dis-*

order (ADHD). New York: Magination Press, 1991.

Rourke, Byron P., and Del Dotto, Jerel E. *Learning Disabilities: A Neuropsychological Perspective*. Thousand Oaks, CA: Sage Publications, 1994.

St. James, Elaine. *Simplify Your Life*. New York: Hyperion, 1994.

Scheiber, Barbara and Jeanne Talpers. *Unlocking Potential: College and Other Choices for Learning Disabled People: A Step-by-Step Guide*. Bethesda, MD: Adler and Adler, 1985.

Schlenger, Sunny. *How to Be Organized in Spite of Yourself.* New York: New American Library, 1989.

Semones, James K. *Effective Study Skills*. Orlando, FL: Harcourt Brace Jovanovich, 1991.

Silver, Susan. *Organized to Be the Best*. Los Angeles: Adams-Hall Publishing, 1989.

Simpson, Eileen. *Reversals: A Personal Account of Victory Over Dyslexia*. Boston: Houghton Mifflin, 1979.

Smith, Sally. *Succeeding Against the Odds*. Los Angeles: Jeremy P. Tarcher, Inc., 1991.

Solden, Sari. *Women with Attention Deficit Disorder*. Green Valley, CA: Underwood Books, 1995.

Stanley, Charles. *The Gift of Forgiveness*. Nashville: Thomas Nelson, 1991.

Tagliaferre, Lewis, and Gary Harbaugh. *Recovery from Loss*. Deerfield Beach, FL: Health Communications, 1990.

Tannen, Deborah. *You Just Don't Understand: Women and Men in Conversation*. New York: William Morrow and Company, 1990.

Thomas, R. Murray. *The Puzzle of Learning Difficulties: Applying a Diagnosis and Treatment Model*. Springfield, IL: Charles C. Thomas Publisher, 1989.

Webb, James T.; Elizabeth A. Meckstroth; and Stephanie Tolan. *Guiding the Gifted Child*. Columbus, OH: Psychology Publishing Company, 1982.

Weiss, Gabrielle, and Lily Torkenberg Hechtman. *Hyperactive Children Grown Up: ADHD in Children, Adolescent, and Adults*. Second Edition. New York: Guilford Press, 1993.

Weiss, Lynn. *Attention Deficit Disorder in Adults*. Dallas, TX: Taylor Publishing Company, 1992.

Wender, Paul. *Attention Deficit Hyperactivity Disorder in Adults*. New York: Oxford Univ. Press, 1995.

_____. *The Hyperactive Child, Adolescent, and Adult: Attention Deficit Disorder through the Lifespan*. New York: Oxford Univ. Press, 1987.

Whiteman, Thomas A., and Michele Novotni. *Adult ADD.: A Reader Friendly Guide to Identifying, Understanding and Treating Adult At-*

tention Deficit Disorder. Colordado Springs: Piñon Press, 1995.

Winston, Stephanie. *Stephanie Winston's Best Organizing Tips.* New York: Simon & Schuster, 1995.

Zametkin, A.; T. Nordahl; M. Gross; A. King; W. Semple; J. Rumsey; S. Hamburger; and S. Cohen, "Cerebral Glucose Metabolism in Adults with Hyperativity of Childhood Onset." *New England Journal of Medicine* 323:1361-66.

Endnotes

Chapter 1: The ABCs of Understanding

1. Edward Hallowell and John Ratey, *Driven to Distraction* (New York: Pantheon, 1994) ix-x.

2. Russell Barkley, *Attention-Deficit Hyperactivity Disorder: A Handbook for Diagnosis and Treatment* (New York: Guilford Press, 1990).

3. Sari Solden, *Women with Attention Deficit Disorder* (Green Valley, CA: Underwood Books, 1995) 24.

4. A. Zametkin, T. Nordahl, M. Gross, A. King, W. Semple, J. Rumsey, S. Hamburger, and S. Cohen, "Cerebral Glucose Metabolism in Adults with Hyperactivity of Childhood Onset," *New England Journal of Medicine* 323: 1361-66.

5. John Ratey, *Challenge Newsletter* 6.1:3.

6. Lynn Weiss, "How Can You Tell Whether You or Someone Else Has ADD?" *Challenge* Nov.-Dec. 1993: 1.

7. Eileen Simpson, *Reversals: A Personal Account of Victory over Dyslexia* (Boston: Houghton Mifflin, 1979) i. Used by permission.

8. Dolores Curran, *Traits of a Healthy Family* (New York: Ballantine Books, 1983).

9. Jill Bloom, *Help Me to Help My Child: A Sourcebook for Parents of Learning Disabled Children* (Boston: Little, Brown and Company, 1990) 19.

10. Kevin Murphy and Suzanne LeVert, *Out of the Fog: Treatment Options and Coping Strategies for Adult Attention Deficit Disorder* (New York: Hyperion, 1995) 28-45.

11. The treatment of dyslexics with anti-motion-sickness medications and related pharmaceutical agents by Dr. Harold Levinson has been described at length in *Smart but Feeling Dumb* (New York: Warner Books, 1984).

Chapter 2: The ABCs of Liking Yourself

1. The Twelve Steps are reprinted with permission of Alcoholics Anonymous World Services, Inc. Permission to reprint the Twelve Steps does not mean that A.A. has reviewed or approved the contents of this publi-

cation, nor that A.A. agrees with the views expressed herein. A.A. is a program of recovery from alcoholism *only*—use of the Twelve Steps in connection with programs and activities which are patterned after A.A., but which address other problems, or in any other non-A.A. context, does not imply otherwise.

2. Lewis Tagliaferre and Gary Harbaugh, *Recovery from Loss* (Deerfield Beach, FL: Health Communications, 1990) 20-21.

3. Thomas Armstrong, *The Myth of the ADD Child: 50 Ways to Improve Your Child's Behavior and Attention Span without Drugs, Labels, or Coercion* (New York: Penguin, 1995).

4. Pesach Krauss and Morrie Goldfinger, *Why Me? Coping with Grief, Loss, and Change* (New York: Bantam Books, 1988) 2.

5. Jeff Campbell and The Clean Team, *Speed Cleaning* (New York: Bantam Doubleday Dell, 1985).

Chapter 3: The ABCs of Coping at Home

1. From "Behind Closed Doors," words and music by Kenny O'Dell, 1973.

2. Solden, *Women with Attention Deficit Disorder* 255.

3. Taken from Elaine K. McEwan, *Attention Deficit Disorder: A Guide for Parents and Educators* (Wheaton, IL: Harold Shaw Publishers, 1996). Concepts and principles adapted from Barbara Y. Whitman and Carla Smith, "Living with a Hyperactive Child: Principles of Families, Family Therapy, and Behavior Management," *Attention Deficit Disorders and Hyperactivity in Children,* ed. P.J. Accardo, T.A. Blondis, and B.Y. Whitman (New York: Marcel Dekker, 1991) 187-211; and from John F. Taylor, *Helping Your Hyperactive/Attention Deficit Child* (Rocklin, CA: Prima Publishing and Communications, 1994) 324-352.

4. Melinda White, "What Adults with ADD Would Like Their Friends, Relatives, and Significant Others to Know," *Challenge* July-Aug. 1994. Reprinted by permission of the author.

5. Rudolph Dreikurs, Shirley Gould, and Raymond J. Corsini, *Family Council: The Dreikurs' Technique for Putting an End to War between Parents and Children (and between Children and Children)* (Chicago: Henry Regnery Company, 1974) 12-14.

6. Irvina Siegel Low, *You Can't Do It All* (New York: Atheneum, 1986) 82ff.

7. David J. Pine, *365 Good Health Habits* (Carson, CA: Hay House, 1994) 26.

8. Edward Hallowell and John Ratey, *Answers to Distraction* (New York: Pantheon, 1994).

9. See Solden, *Women with Attention Deficit Disorder.*

Chapter 4: The ABCs of Keeping on Track

1. Don Aslett, *How to Have a 48-Hour Day* (Cincinnati: Betterway Books, 1996) 115.

2. Quoted in *Women's Wisdom through the Ages* (Wheaton, IL: Harold Shaw Publishers, 1994) 35.

Chapter 5: The ABCs of Working

1. Mihaly Csikszentmihalyi, *Flow: The Psychology of Optimal Experience* (New York: Harper Perennial, 1990).

2. Salvatore Mannuzza, Rachel G. Klein, Abram Bessler, Patricia Malloy, and Maia LaPadula, "Adult Outcome of Hyperactive Boys," *Archives of General Psychiatry* 50 (July 1993).

3. Peter Drucker, *Adventures of a Bystander* (New York: Harper & Row, 1979) 255.

4. Maria Laqueur and Donna Dickinson, *Breaking Out of 9 to 5* (Princeton: Peterson's, 1994) 58.

5. Barry and Linda Gale, *Stay or Leave* (New York: Harper & Row, 1989) 41.

6. Ralph Keyes, *Timelock: How Life Got So Hectic and What You Can Do About It* (New York: HarperCollins, 1991) 204.

7. Adapted from Sunny Schlenger, *How to Be Organized in Spite of Yourself* (New York: New American Library, 1989).

8. Kahlil Gibran, *The Prophet* (New York: Alfred A. Knopf, 1923) 28.

Chapter 6: The ABCs of Lifelong Learning

1. James T. Webb, Elizabeth A. Meckstroth, and Stephanie Tolan, *Guiding the Gifted Child* (Columbus, OH: Psychology Publishing Company, 1982) 52.

2. Webb, et al., *Guiding the Gifted Child.*

3. Thomas Armstrong, *Seven Kinds of Smart* (New York: Penguin Books, 1993).

4. Quoted in Armstrong, *Seven Kinds of Smart* 177.

5. Armstrong, *Seven Kinds of Smart* 183.

6. James K. Semones, *Effective Study Skills* (Fort Wort, TX: Harcourt Brace Jovanovich, 1991) 30-36.

Chapter 7: The ABCs of Living Fully

1. Richard Foster, *Celebration of Discipline* (San Francisco: HarperSan Francisco, 1988) 143.

2. Charles Stanley, *The Gift of Forgiveness* (Nashville: Thomas Nelson, 1991).

3. David Grudermeyer, Rebecca Grudermeyer, and Lerissa Nancy Patrick. *Sensible Self-Help: The First Road Map for the Healing Journey* (Del Mar, CA: Willingness Works Press, 1995) 404.

4. Harvey Cox, *The Feast of Fools* (Cambridge, MA: Harvard University Press, 1969) 10.

5. Ronald Klug, *How to Keep a Spiritual Journal* (Minneapolis: Augsburg, 1993) 11.

6. Thomas Kelly, *The Eternal Promise* (New York: Harper & Row, 1966) 72.

7. Stuart Briscoe, *What Works When Life Doesn't* (Wheaton, IL: Victor Books, 1983).

8. Carolyn Deitering, *I Am a Pilgrim Child* (Mystic, CT: Twenty-Third Publications, 1992) 37. Reprinted by permission of the author.

9. Foster, *Celebration of Discipline* 33.

10. "A Prayer Sampler," *Lutheran Women Today* May 1996: 2-4.

11. Foster, *Celebration of Discipline* 27.

12. Thomas Merton, *Spiritual Direction and Meditation* (Collegeville, MN: Liturgical Press, 1960) 65.

13. Foster, *Celebration of Discipline* 17.

14. Foster, *Celebration of Discipline* 32.

15. H. Jackson Browne, Jr., *Life's Little Instruction Book* (Nashville: Rutledge Hill, 1992).

16. Grudermeyer, et al., *Sensible Self-Help.*

17. Grudermeyer, et al., *Sensible Self-Help* 257.

Index